AF470536

IDEAS LEAVE OBJECTS STANDING

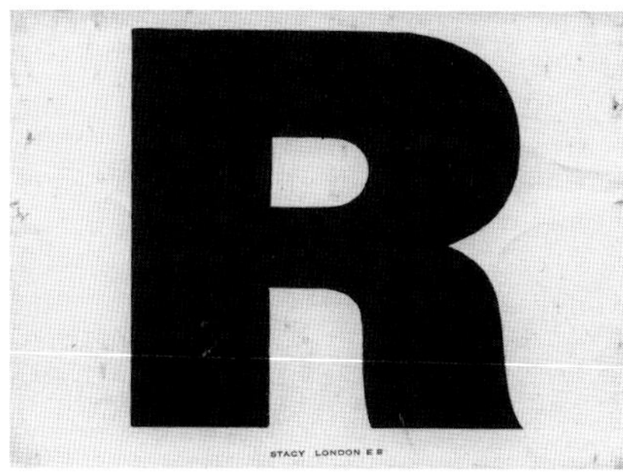

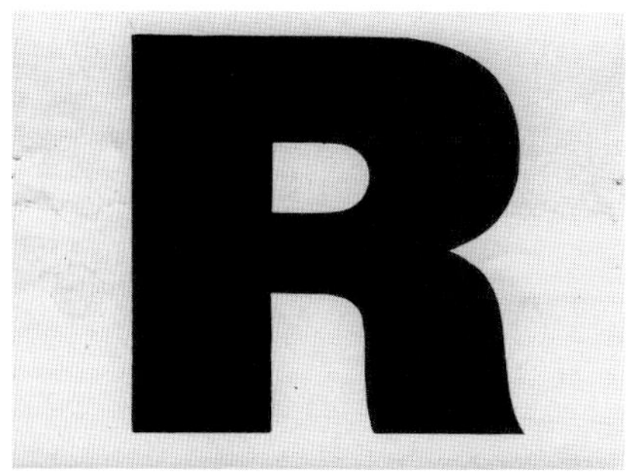

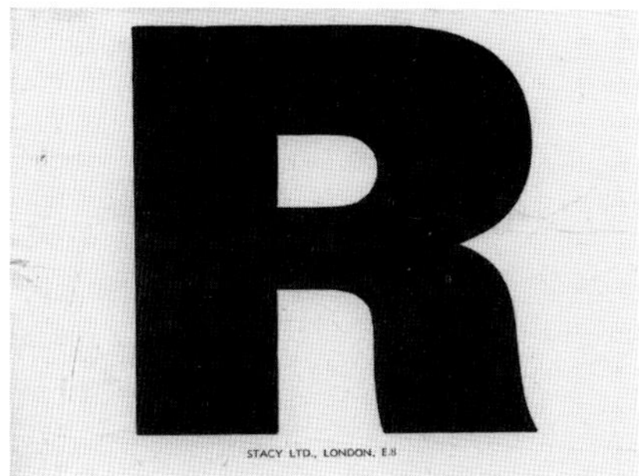

The Three R's

IDEAS LEAVE OBJECTS STANDING

David Bellingham

platform projects
BALTIC
2005

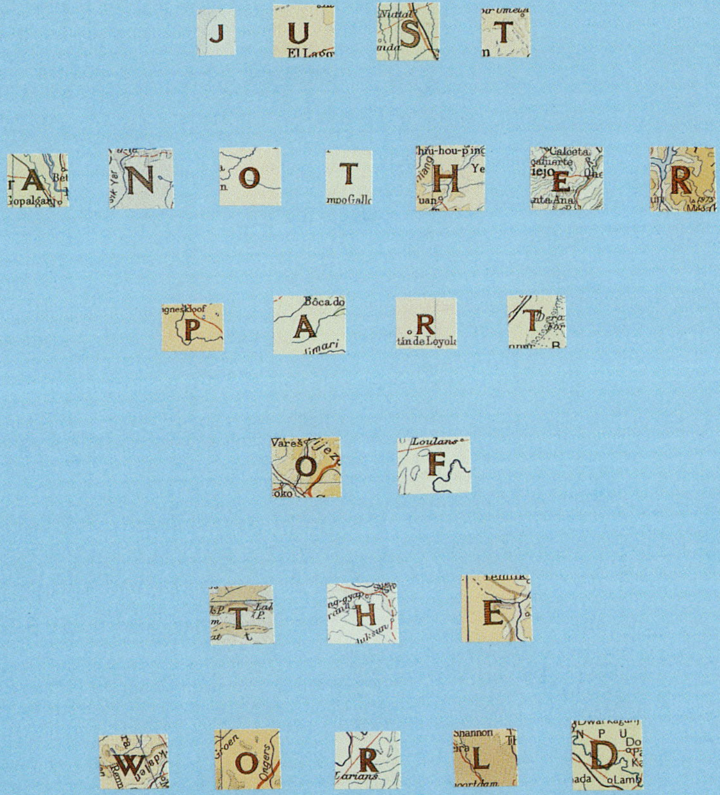

J U S T

A N O T H E R

P A R T

O F

T H E

W O R L D

north

left

right

south

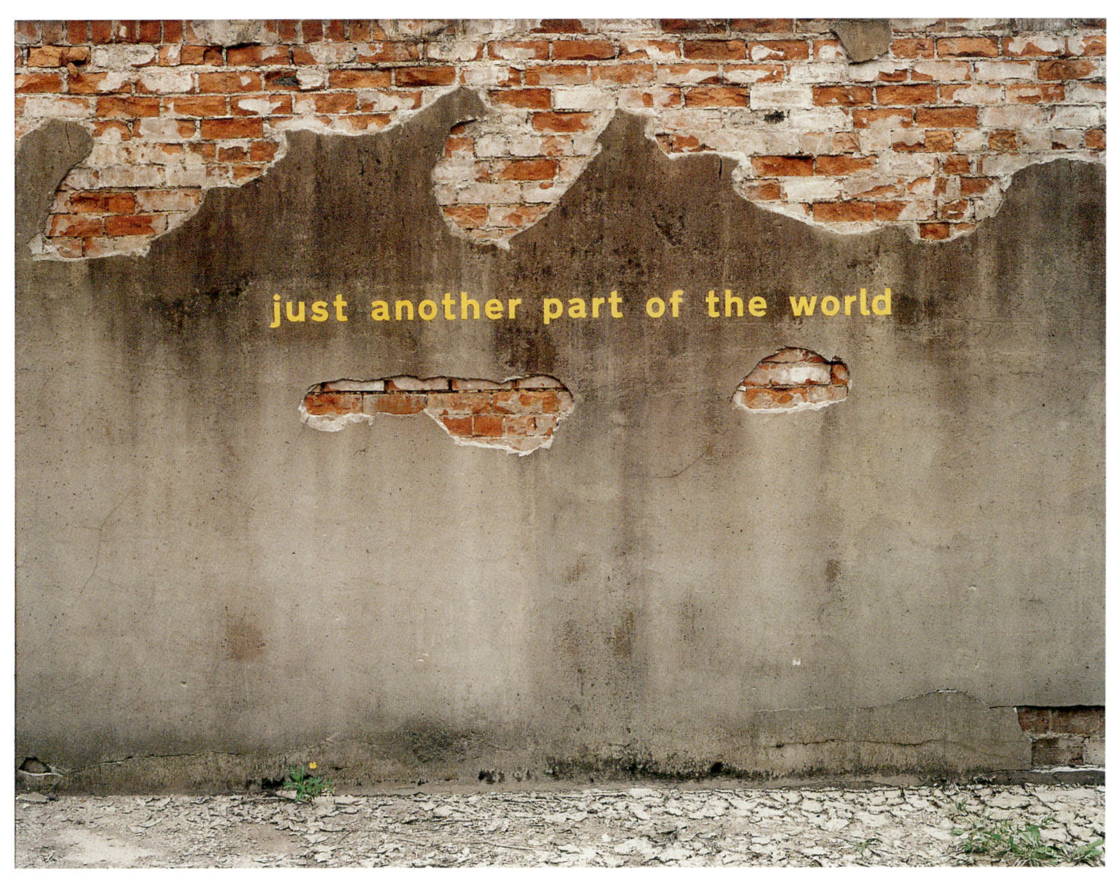
just another part of the world

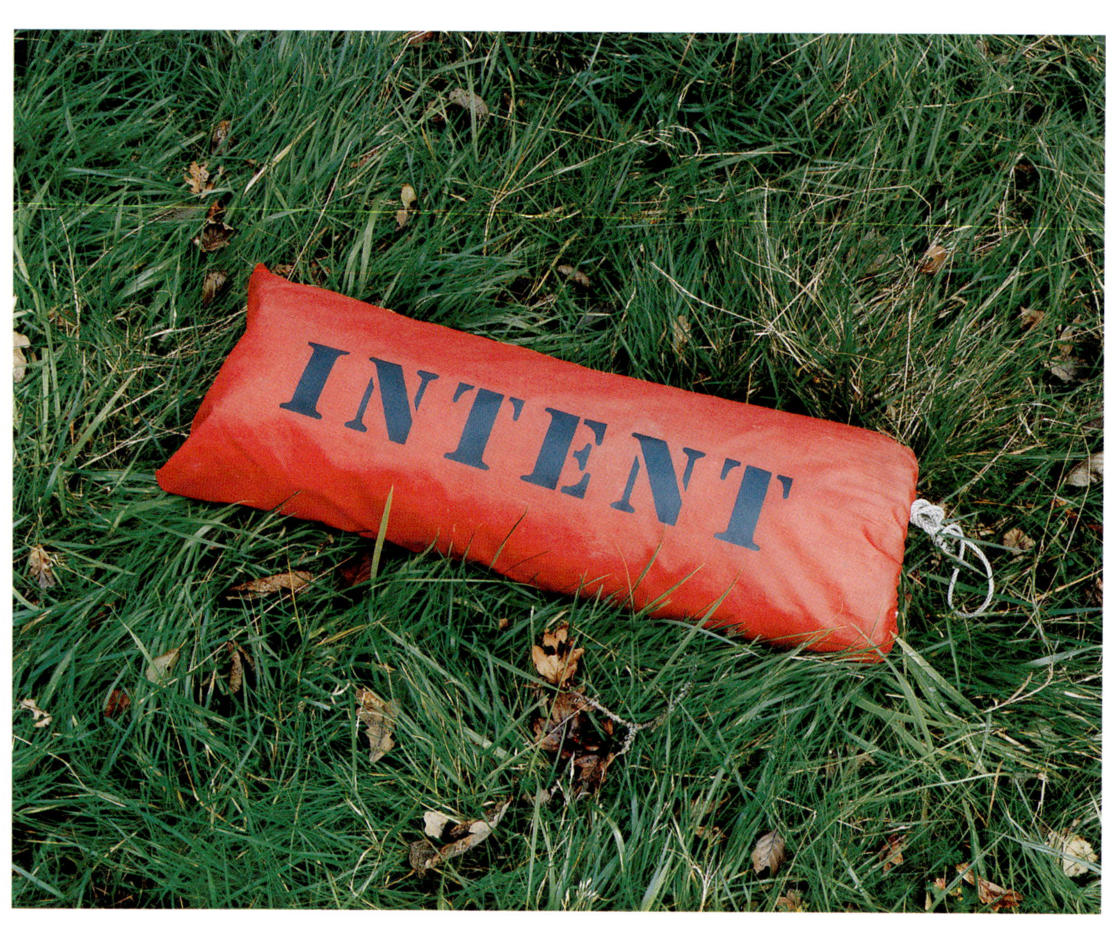
INTENT

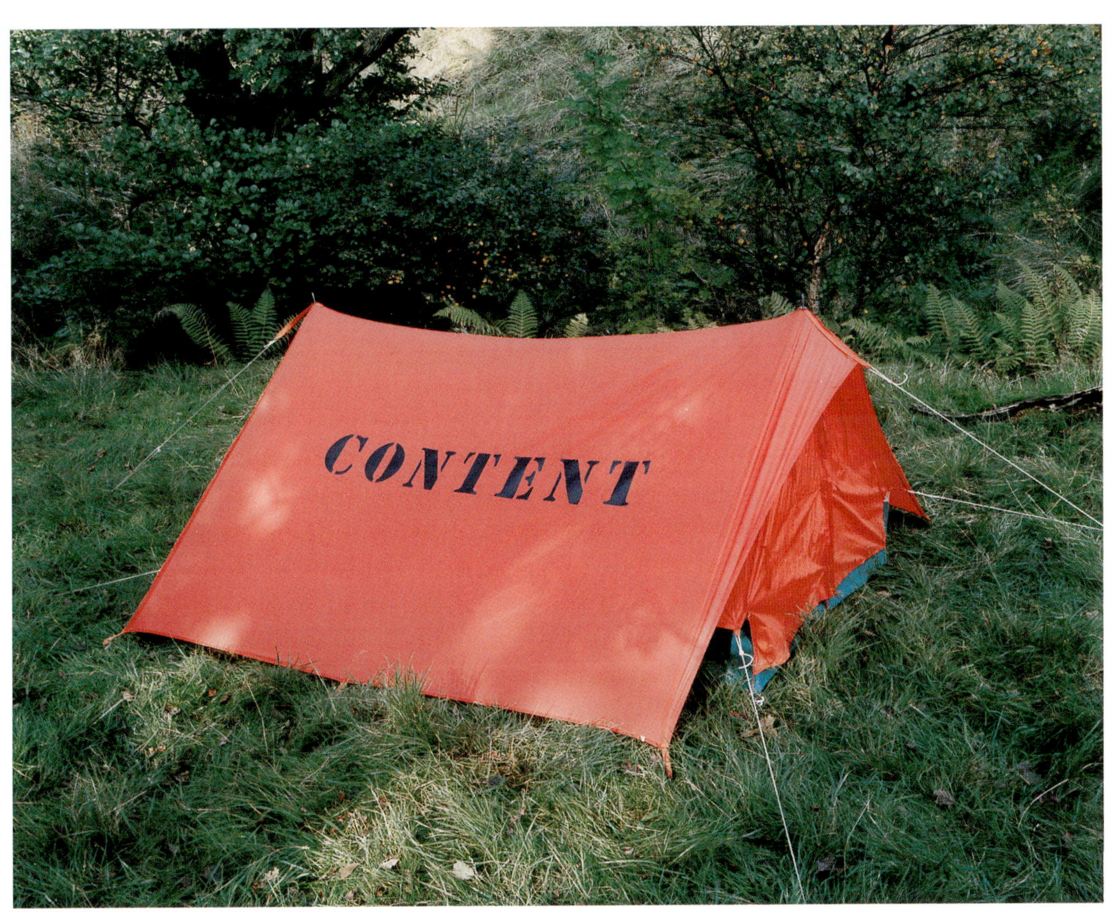
CONTENT

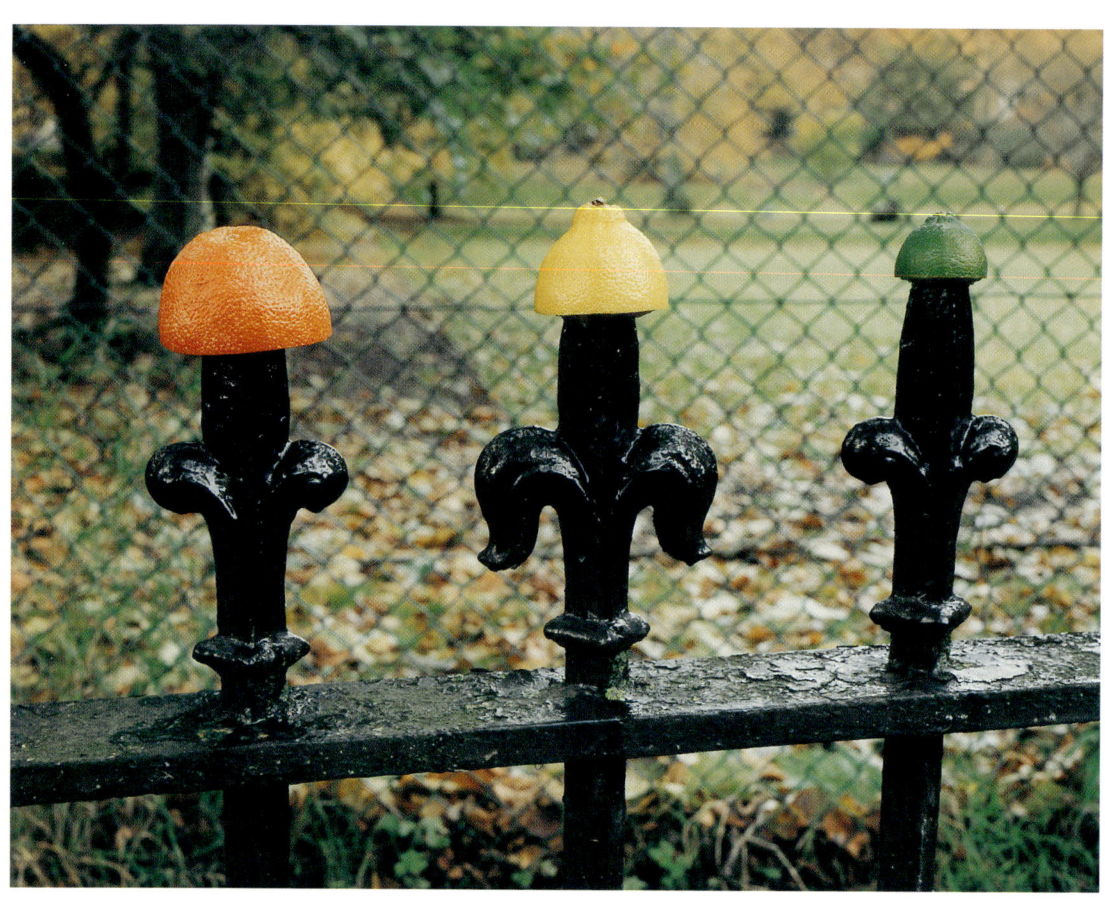

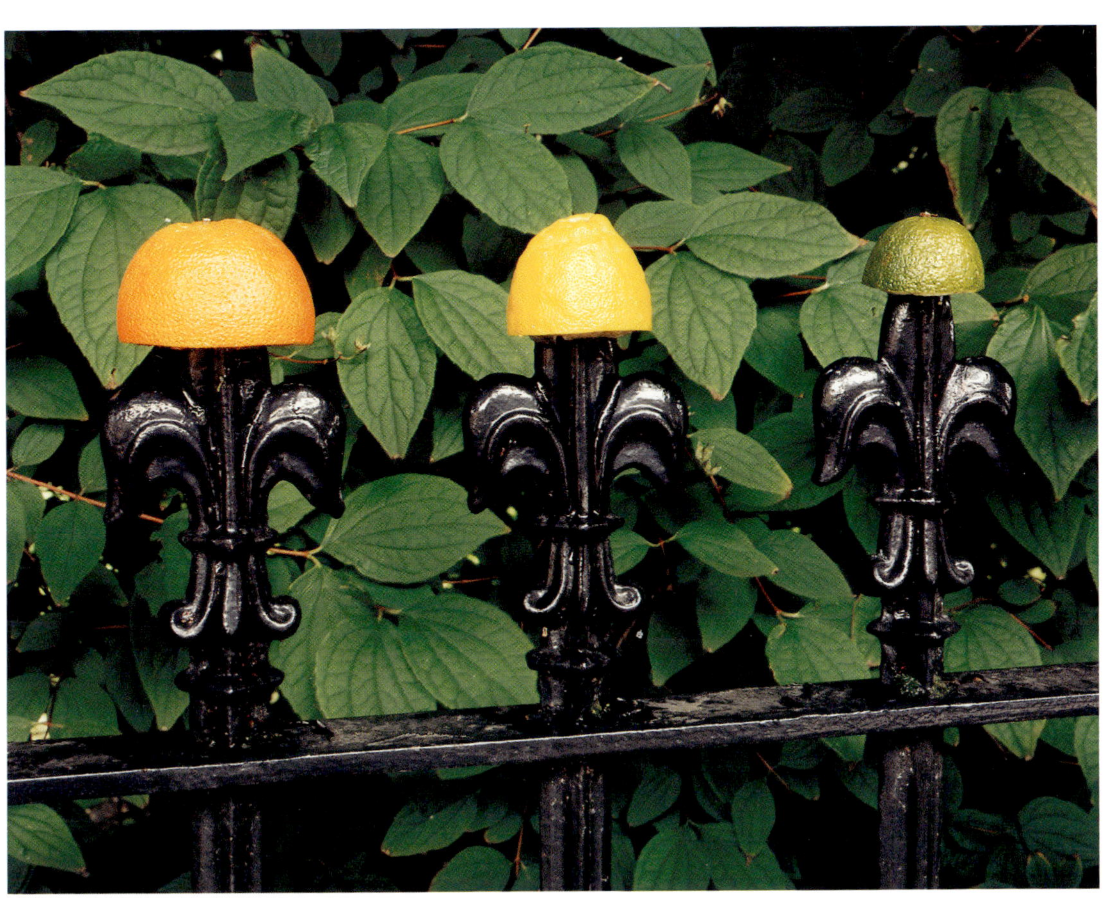

lemon
yellow
lemon

lime
green
lime

orange
orange

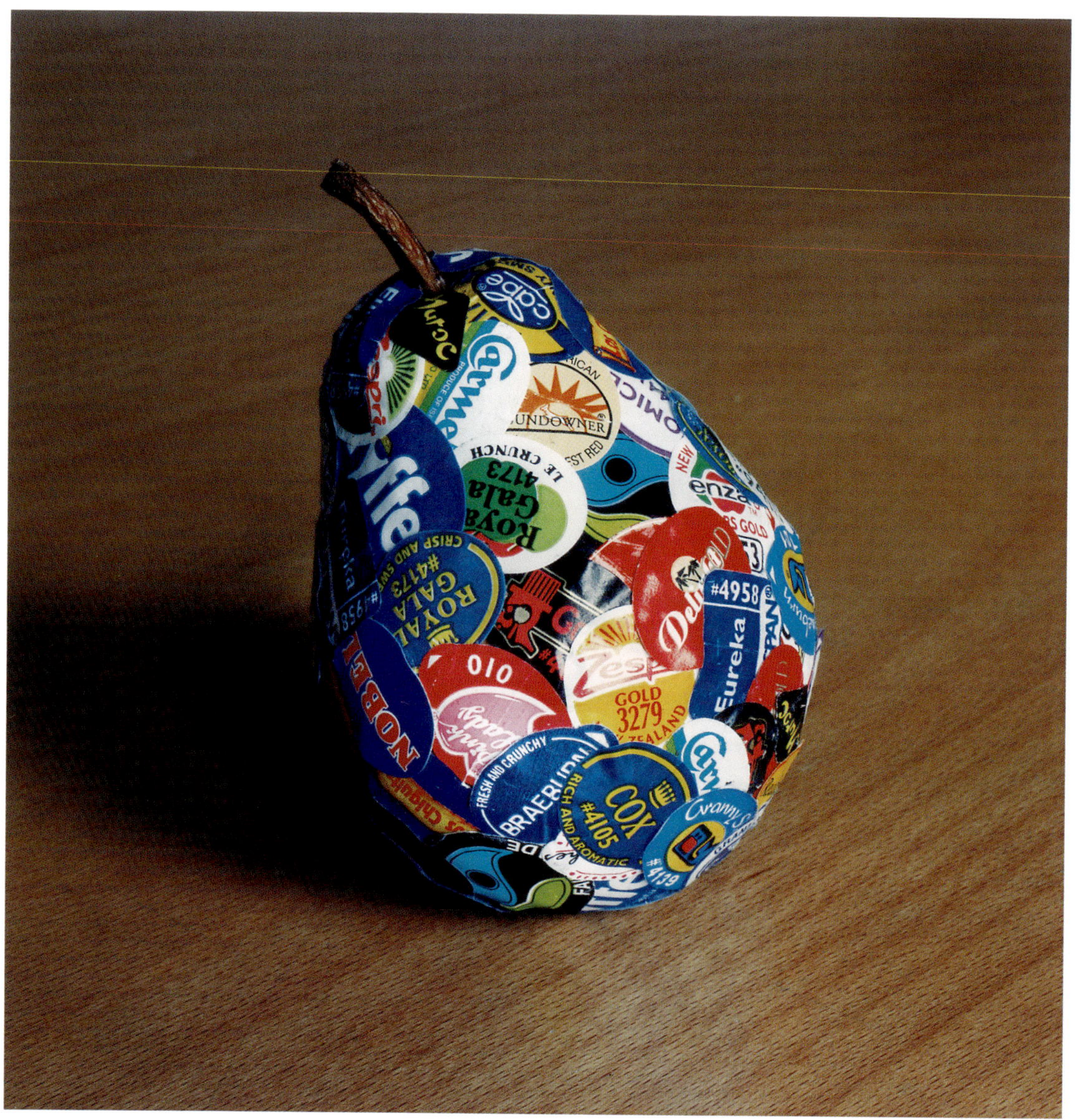
cape
LE CRUNCH
Royal Gala
4173
ROYAL GALA
#4173
#4958
Eureka
GOLD
3279
010
FRESH AND CRUNCHY
COX
#4105
RICH AND AROMATIC
enza

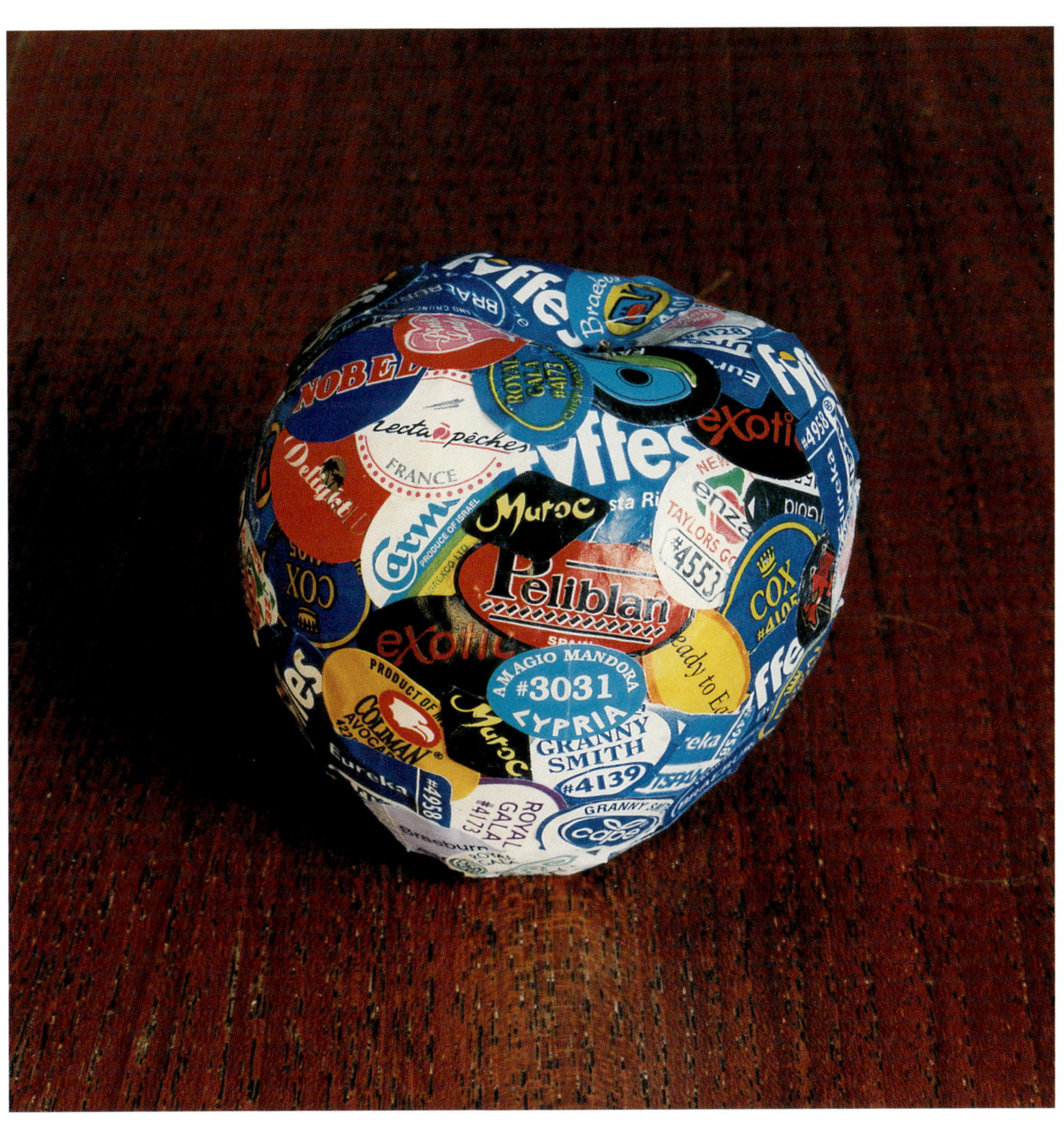

Collage (after Jiří Kolář)

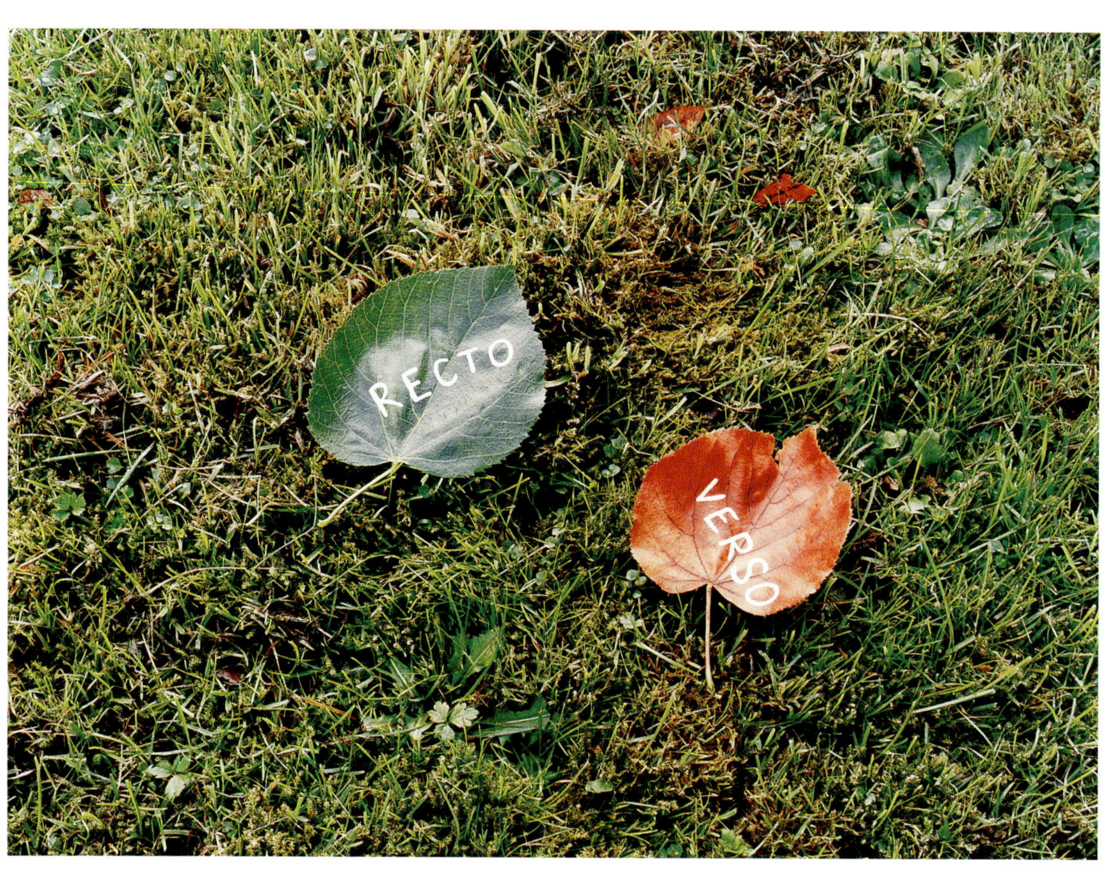
RECTO
VERSO

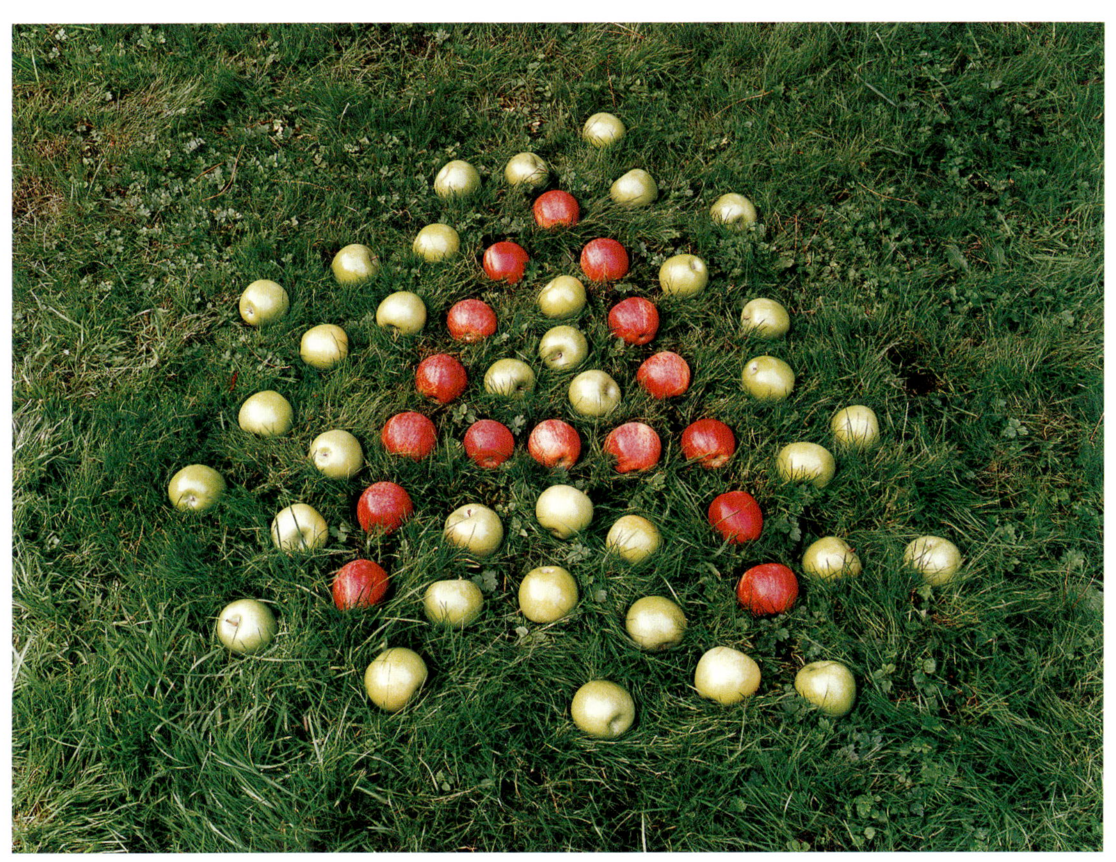

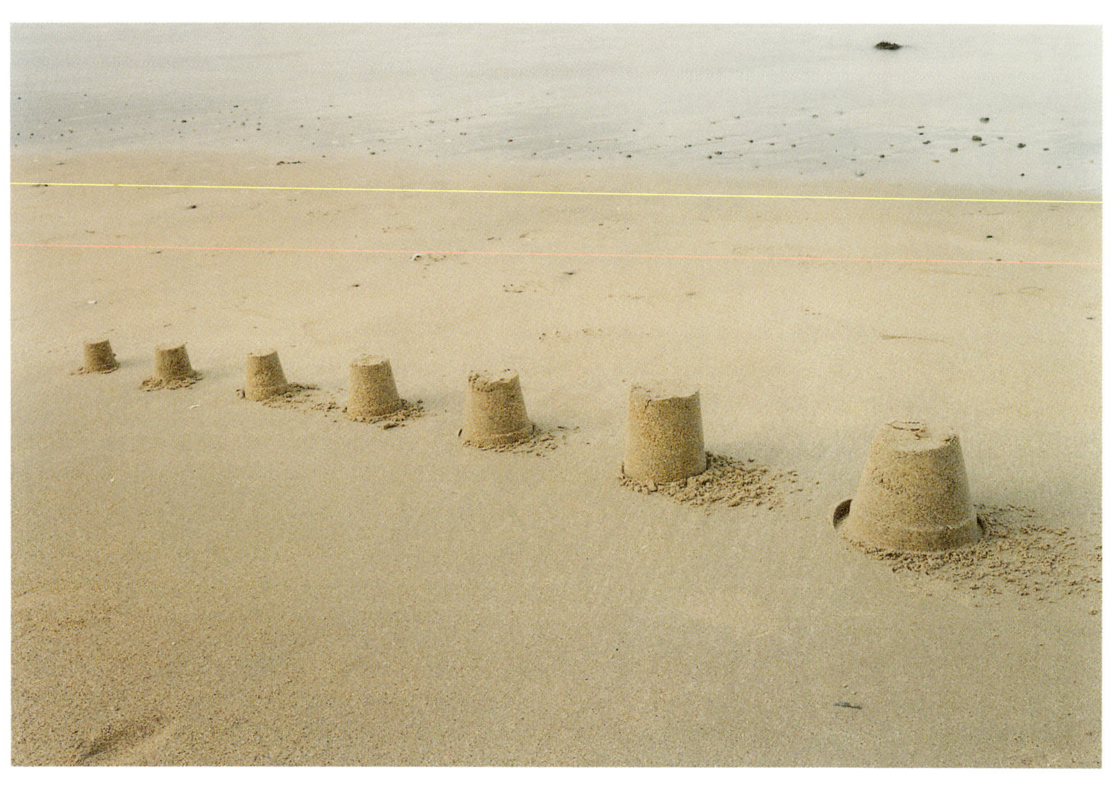

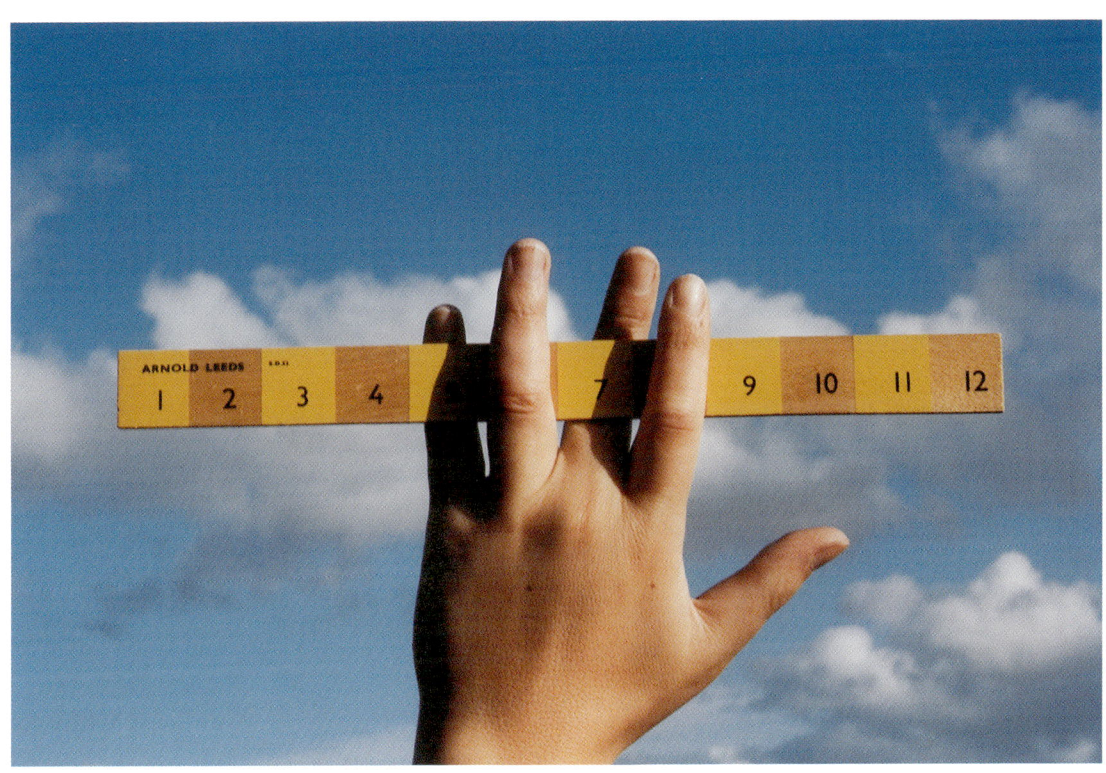
ARNOLD LEEDS
1 2 3 4 7 9 10 11 12

Cruise: A Wandering Journey In Search Of An Enemy

/grain/missiles/grain/missiles/grain/missile
missiles/grain/missiles/grain/missiles/grain
/grain/missiles/grain/missiles/grain/missile
missiles/grain/missiles/grain/missiles/grain
/grain/missiles/grain/missiles/grain/missile
missiles/grain/missiles/grain/missiles/grain
/grain/missiles/grain/missiles/grain/missile
missiles/grain/missiles/grain/missiles/grain
/grain/missiles/grain/missiles/grain/missile
missiles/grain/missiles/grain/missiles/grain
/grain/missiles/grain/missiles/grain/missile
missiles/grain/missiles/grain/missiles/grain
/grain/missiles/grain/missiles/grain/missile
missiles/grain/missiles/grain/missiles/grain
/grain/missiles/grain/missiles/grain/missile
missiles/grain/missiles/grain/missiles/grain
/grain/missiles/grain/missiles/grain/missile
missiles/grain/missiles/grain/missiles/grain
/grain/missiles/grain/missiles/grain/missile
missiles/grain/missiles/grain/missiles/grain
/grain/missiles/grain/missiles/grain/missile
missiles/grain/missiles/grain/missiles/grain
/grain/missiles/grain/missiles/grain/missile
missiles/grain/missiles/grain/missiles/grain
/grain/missiles/grain/missiles/grain/missile
missiles/grain/missiles/grain/missiles/grain
/grain/missiles/grain/missiles/grain/missile
missiles/grain/missiles/grain/missiles/grain
/grain/missiles/grain/missiles/grain/missile
missiles/grain/missiles/grain/missiles/grain
/grain/missiles/grain/missiles/grain/missile
missiles/grain/missiles/grain/missiles/grain
/grain/missiles/grain/missiles/grain/missile
missiles/grain/missiles/grain/missiles/grain
/grain/missiles/grain/missiles/grain/missile
missiles/grain/missiles/grain/missiles/grain
/grain/missiles/grain/missiles/grain/missile
missiles/grain/missiles/grain/missiles/grain
/grain/missiles/grain/missiles/grain/missile
missiles/grain/missiles/grain/missiles/grain
/grain/missiles/grain/missiles/grain/missile
missiles/grain/missiles/grain/missiles/grain
/grain/missiles/grain/missiles/grain/missile
missiles/grain/missiles/grain/missiles/grain
/grain/missiles/grain/missiles/grain/missile

green field
brown field

oil field
battle field

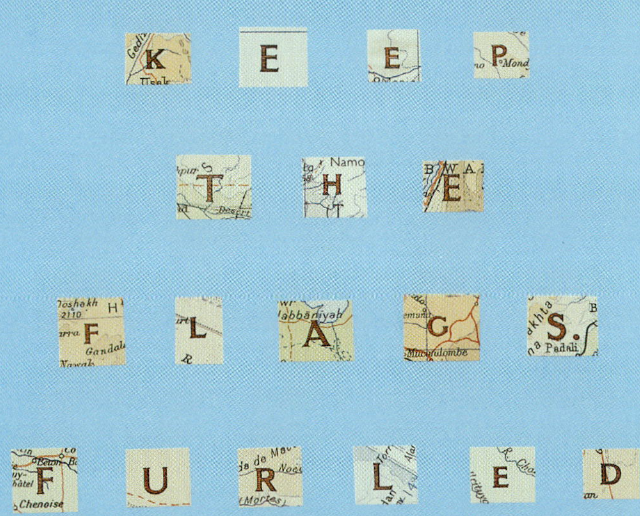
K E E P
T H E
F L A G S.
F U R L E D

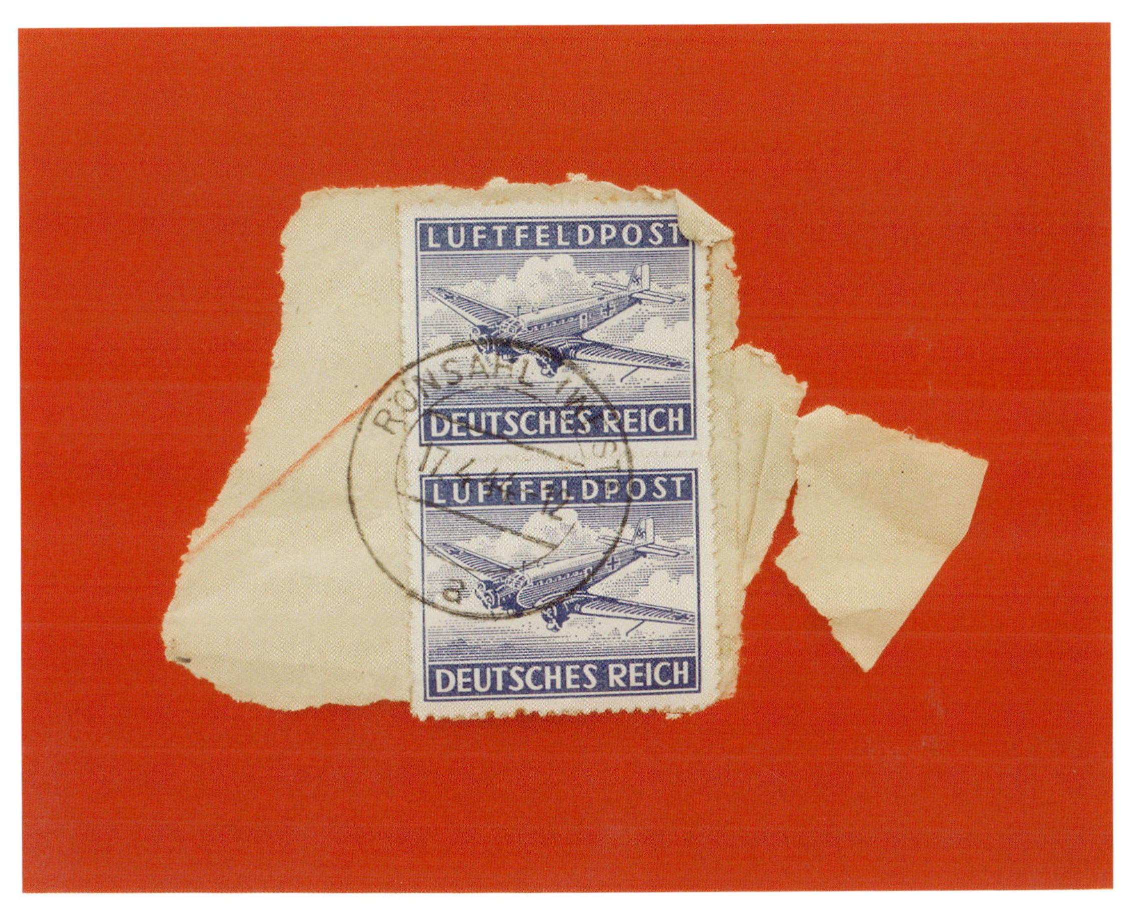

LUFTFELDPOST
DEUTSCHES REICH
LUFTFELDPOST
DEUTSCHES REICH

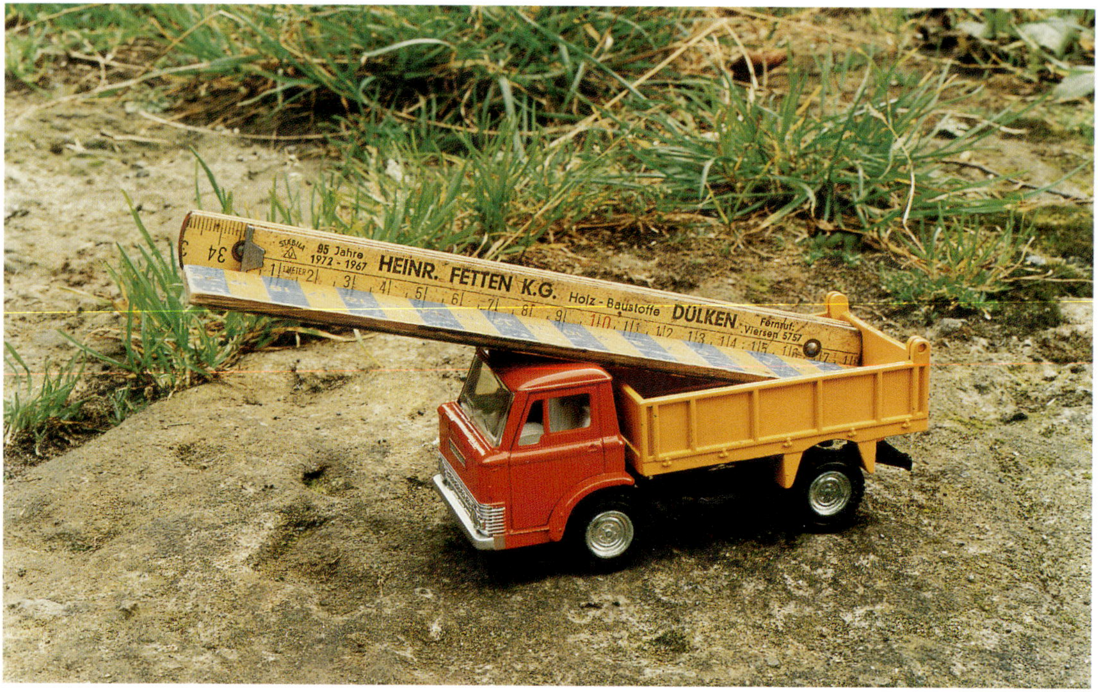

HEINR. FETTEN K.G.
Holz - Baustoffe
DULKEN

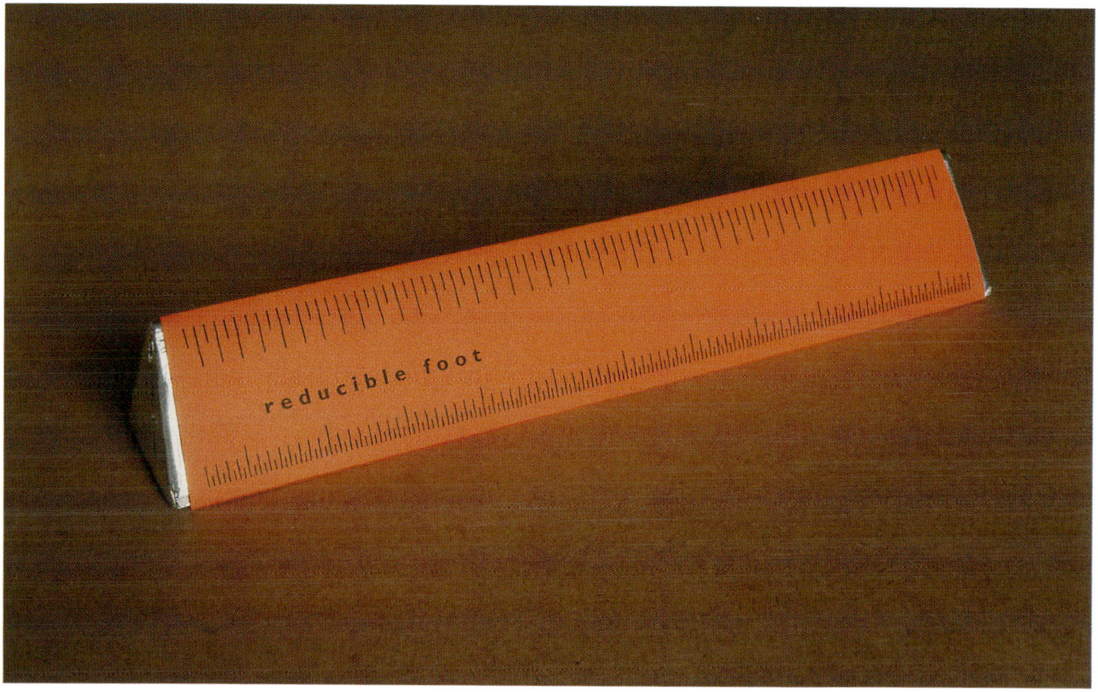

reducible foot

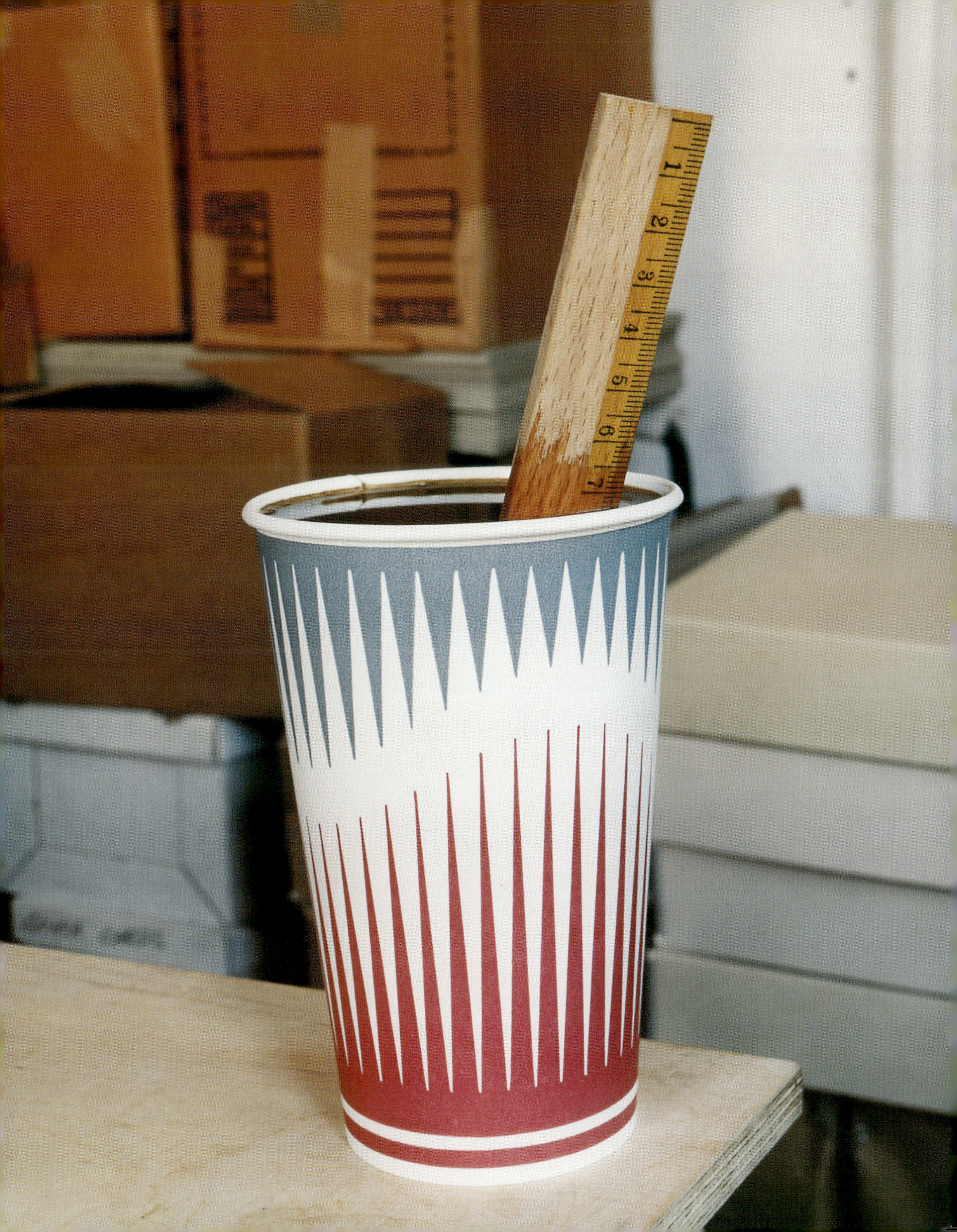

NOT
ONLY
BLACK
AND
WHITE

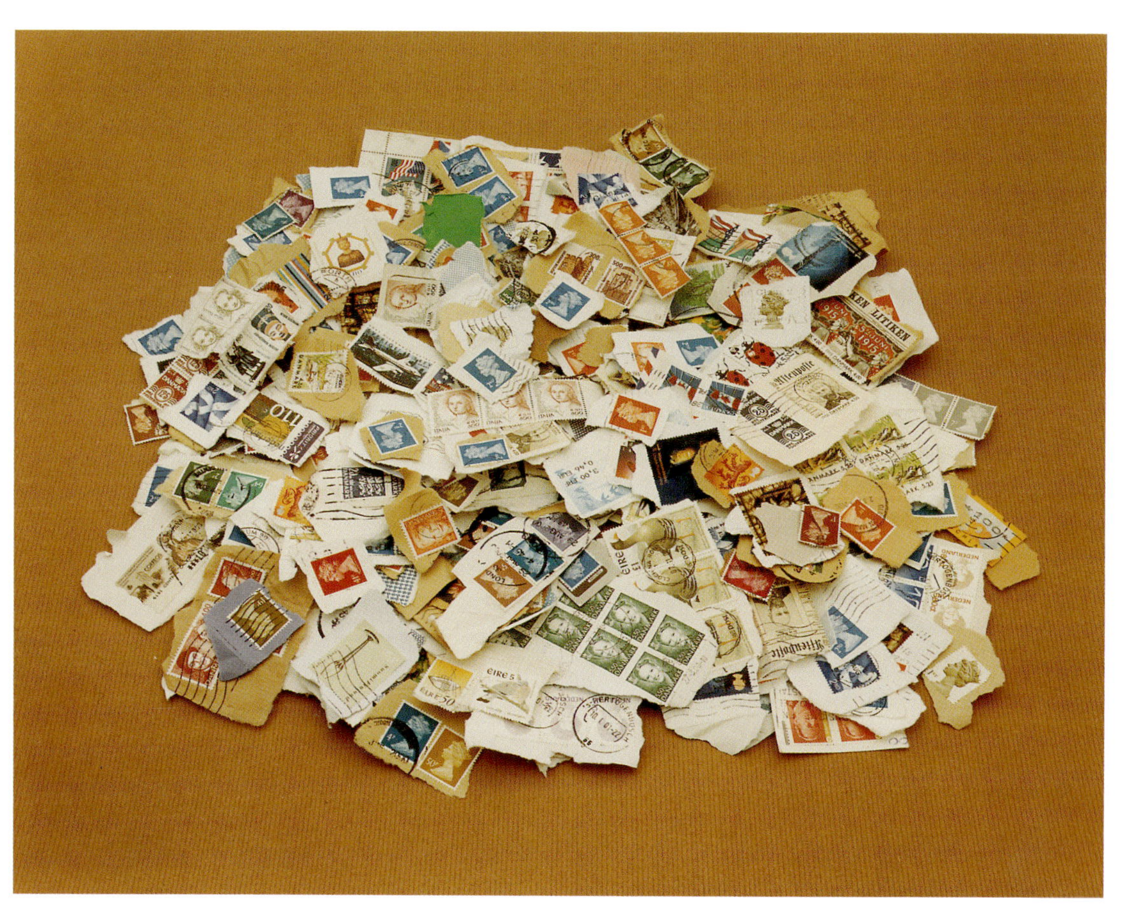

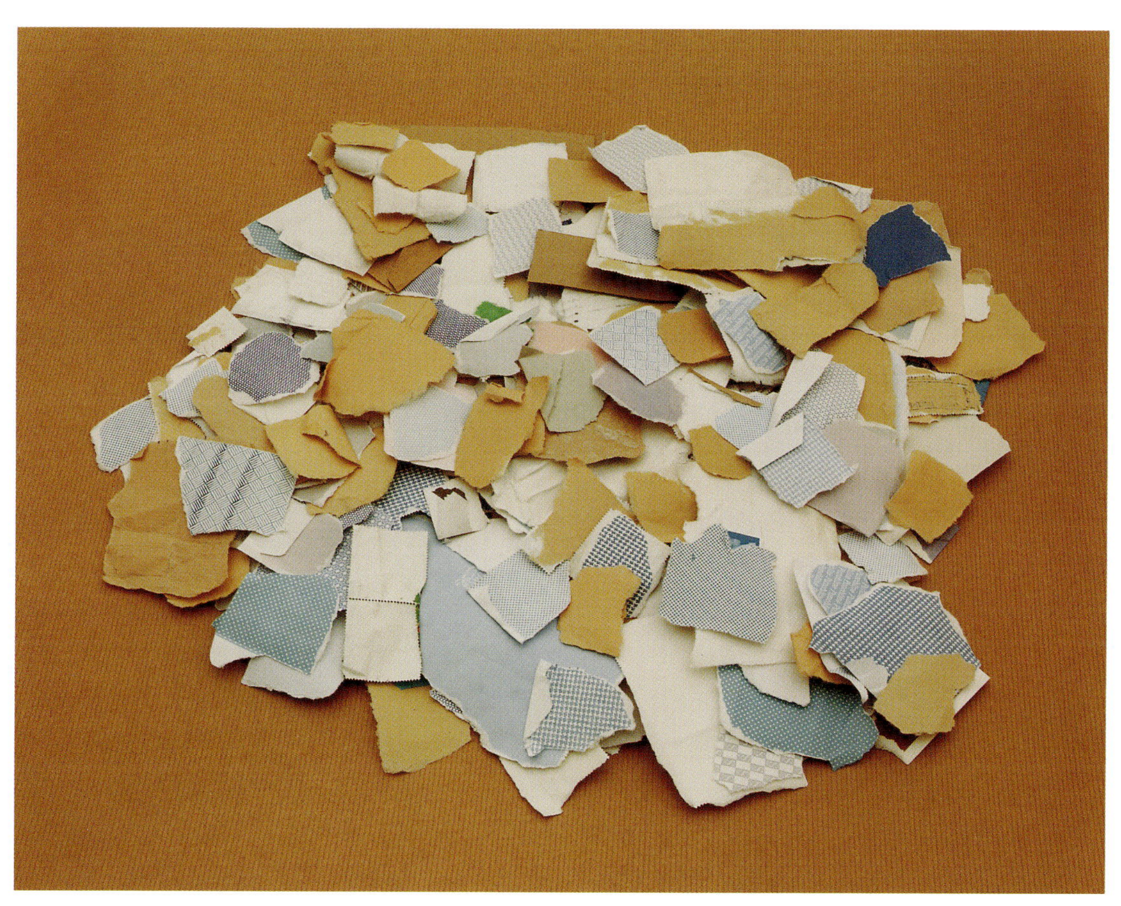

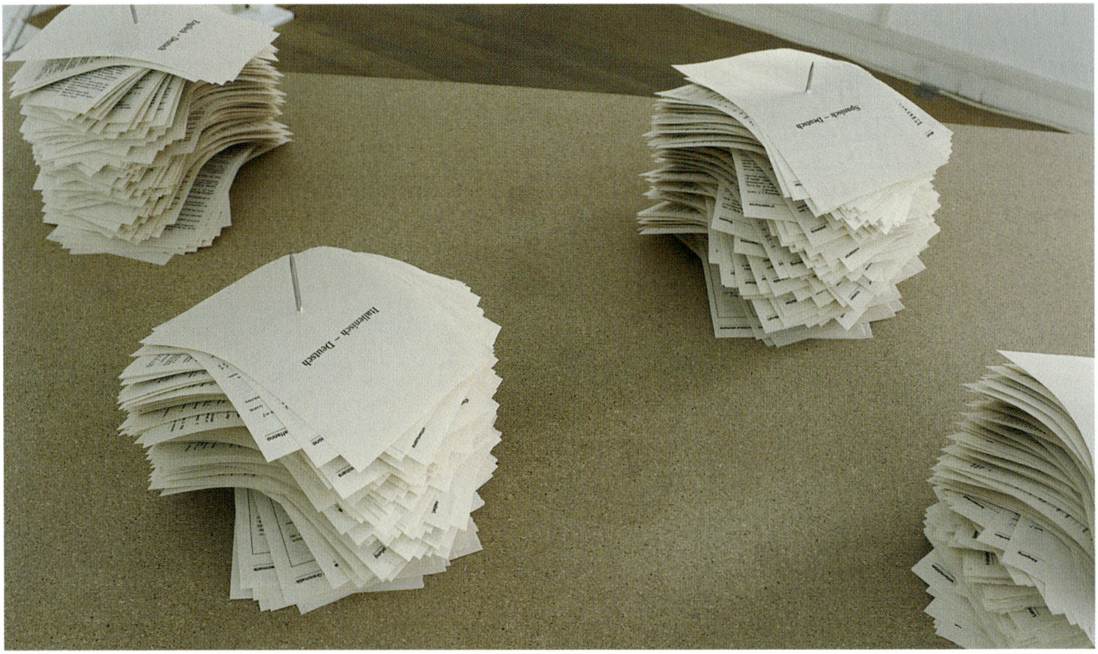

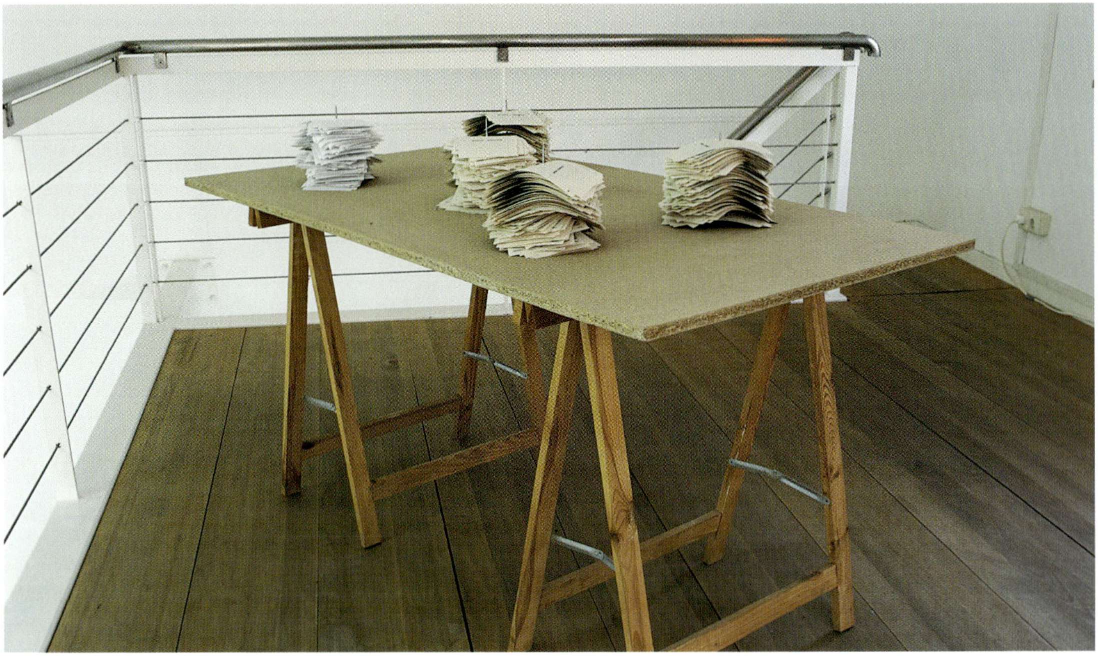

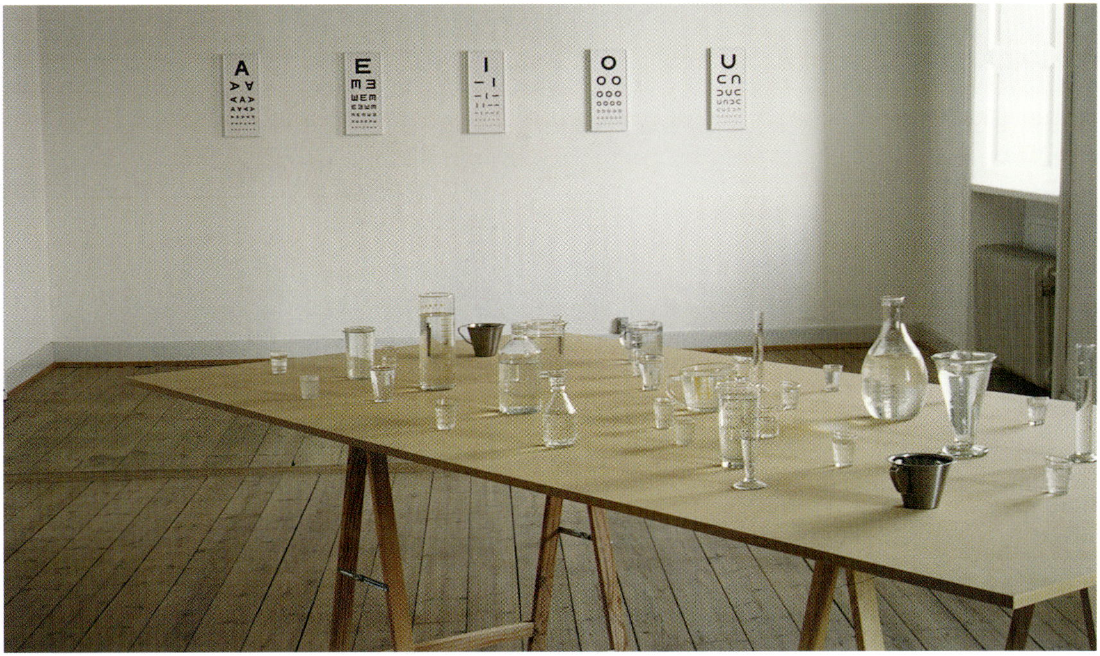

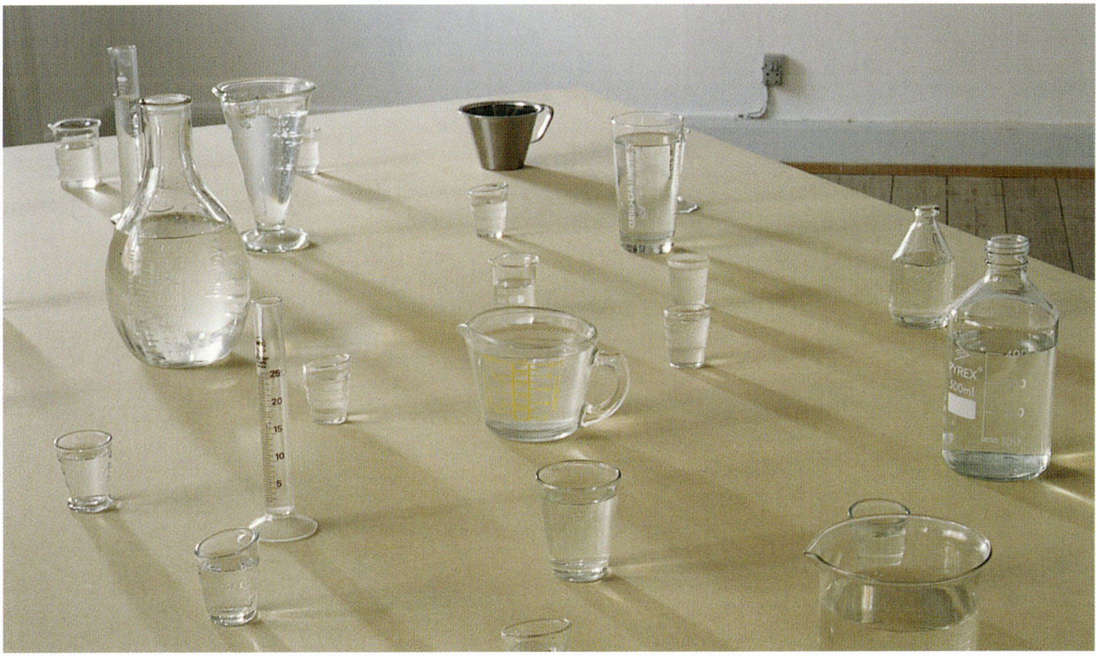

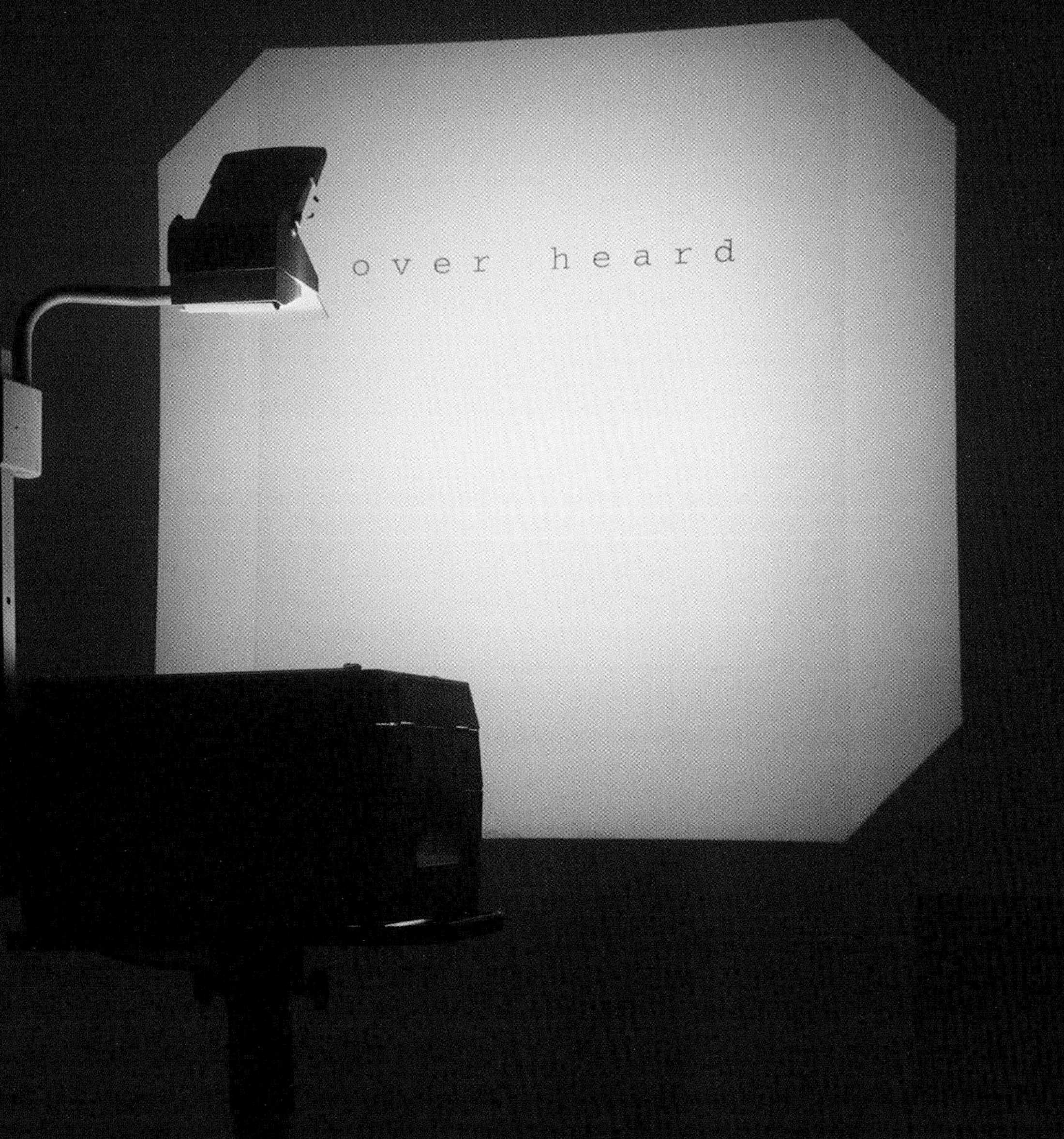
over heard

a weight

of words

as light

as paper

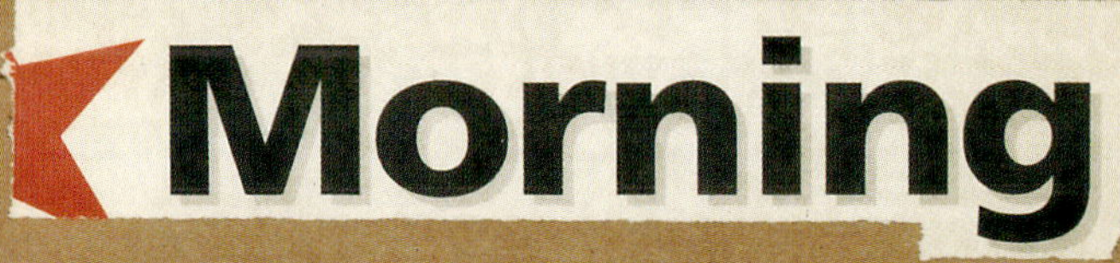

Evening

Daily

DAILY

DAILY

Daily

DAILY

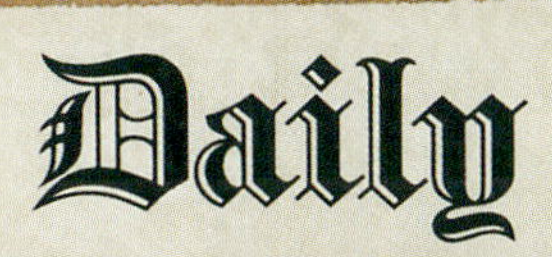

Daily

Daily

WEEKLY

CARTE VALLOT

CARTE GÉNÉRALE
DU
MASSIF DU MONT-BLANC

à l'échelle de 1 : 50.000[E]

en une feuill

Mont Blanc
savon - soap

Ch. VAL AT

S Courmayeur

Chamonix

Vallorcine — Saint-Gervais-les-Bains

GIRARD BARRÈRE ET THOMAS
GÉOGRAPHES-ÉDITEURS
17, Rue de Buci
PARIS-6

Le Monde
Le Monde
Le Monde
Le Monde
Le Monde
Le Monde
Le Monde
Le Monde

IDEAS
made rather than found

THINGS

found rather than made

ART

a modest lamp flickering against the wind

FORM

found on the doorstep shivering in a cardboard box

KNOWLEDGE

a field within the plain of understanding

KNOW-HOW

a pencil in one hand a hammer in the other

GREENWICH • EVERY CLOCK RESIDES IN ITS OWN

TIME
is our habitat

TIME

is what is happening in the sky

HISTORY

is what is happening on the ground

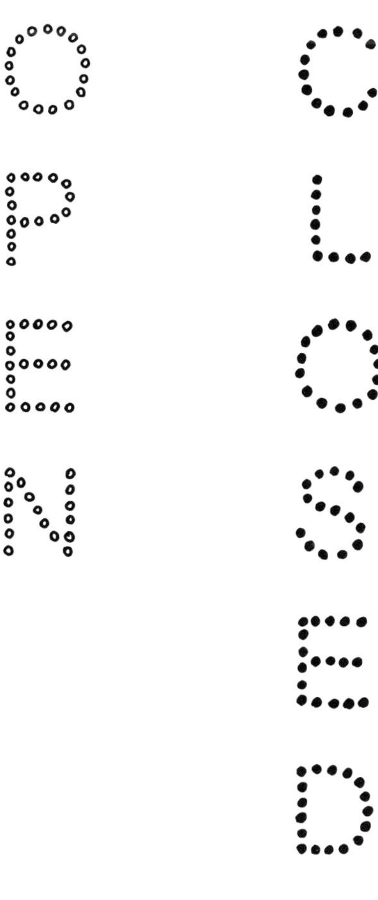
OPEN
CLOSED

things over signs

w
orking

wo
rking

wor
king

work
ing

worki
ng

workin
g

p
laying

pl
aying

pla
ying

play
ing

playi
ng

playin
g

javelin   the line
discus   the surface
shot-put   the solid

river   the line
lake   the surface
ocean   the volume

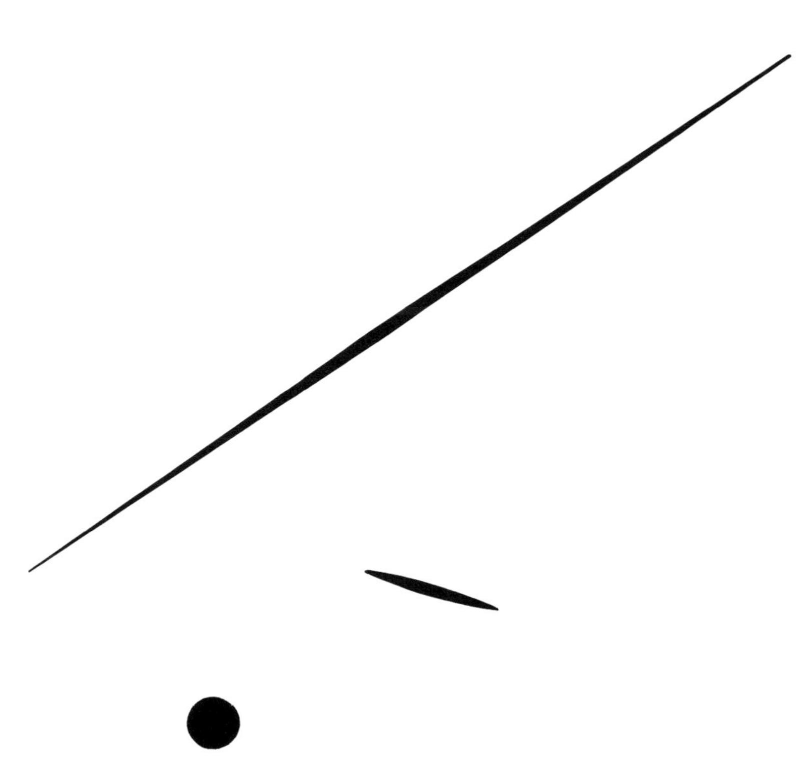

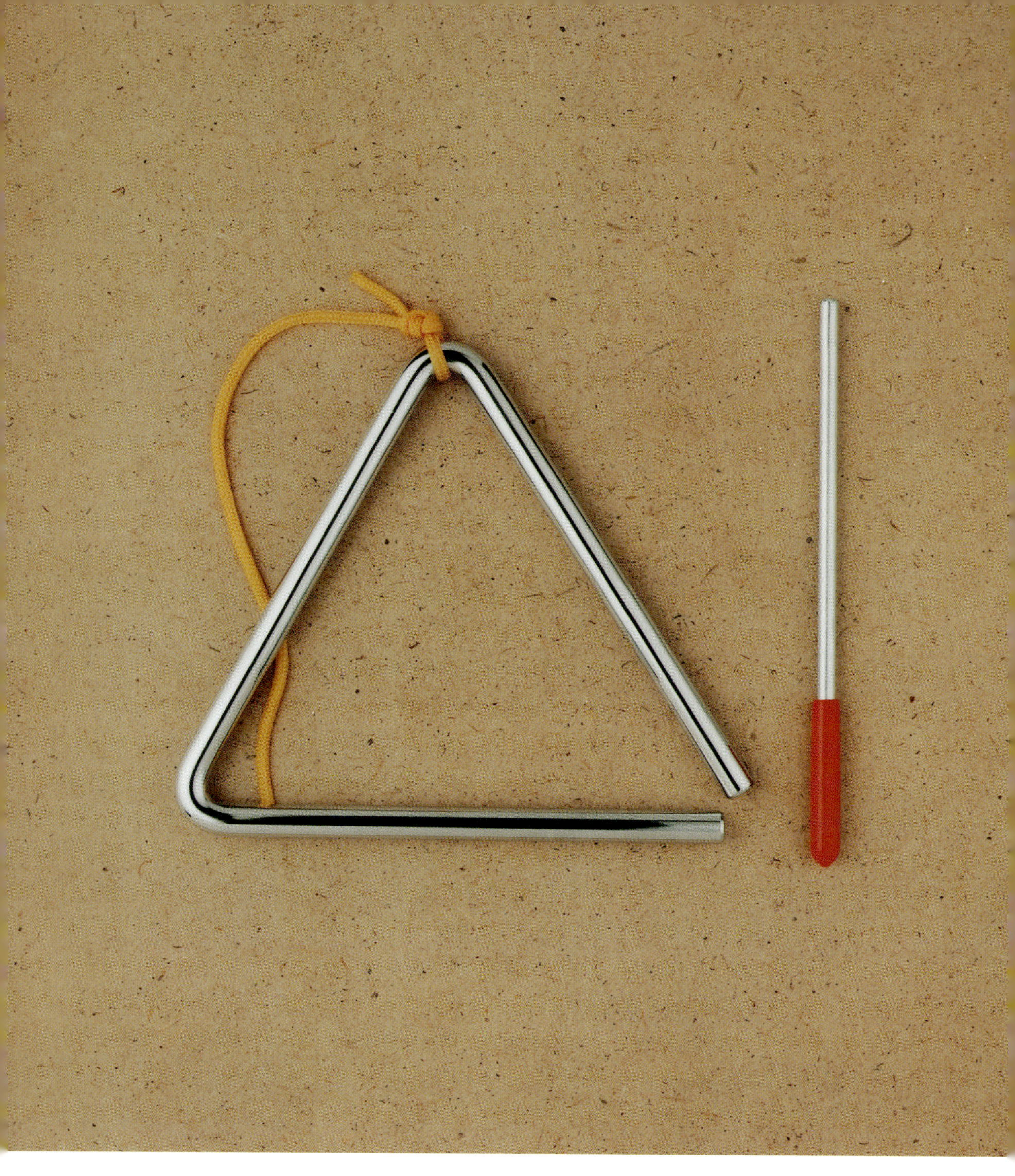

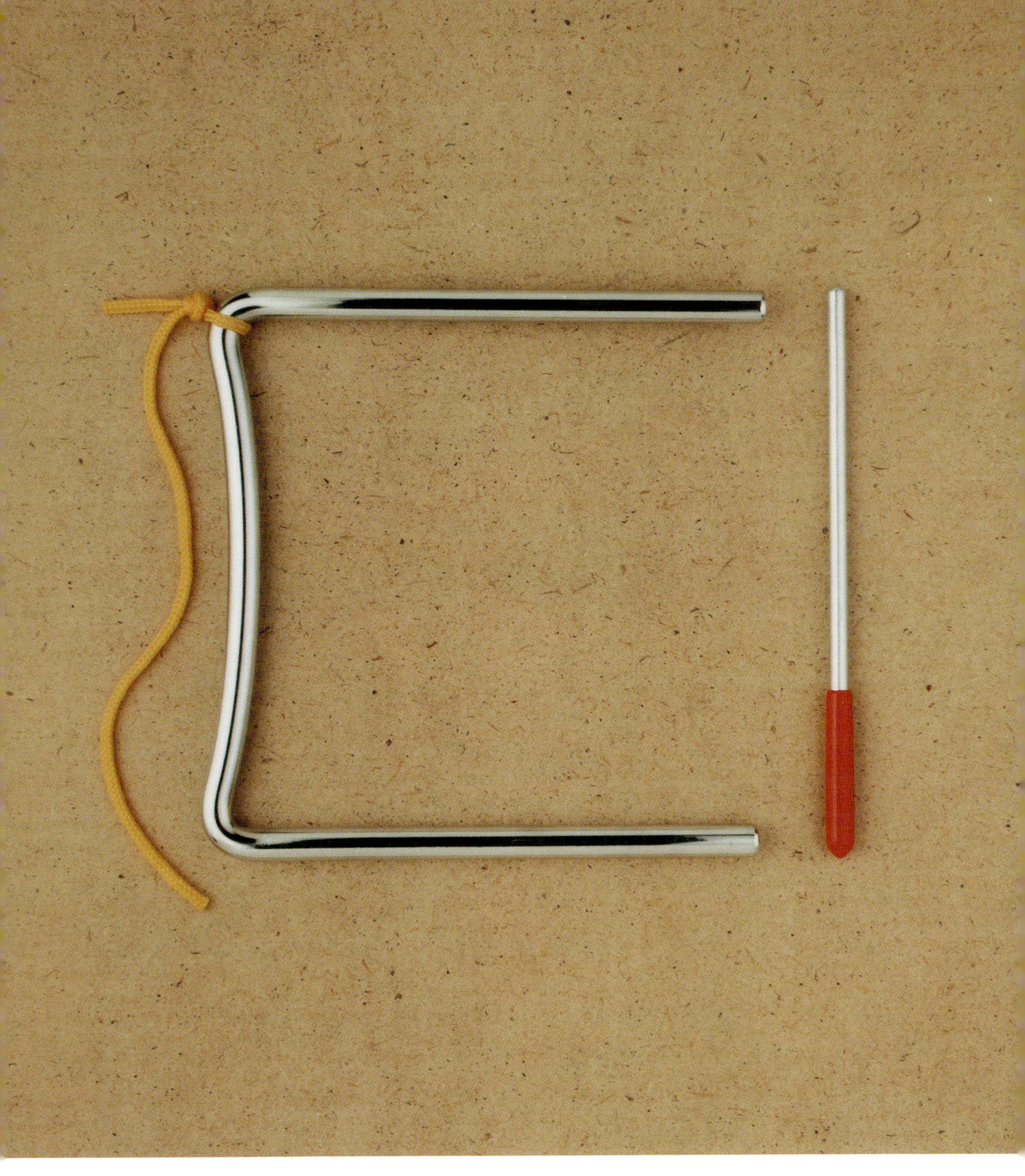

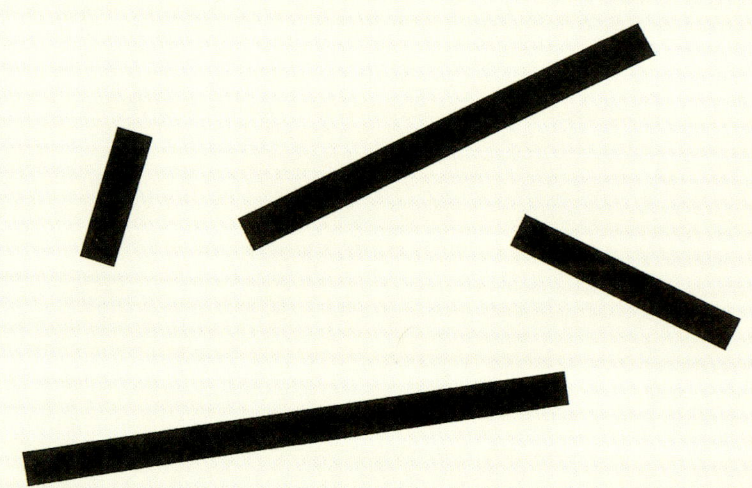

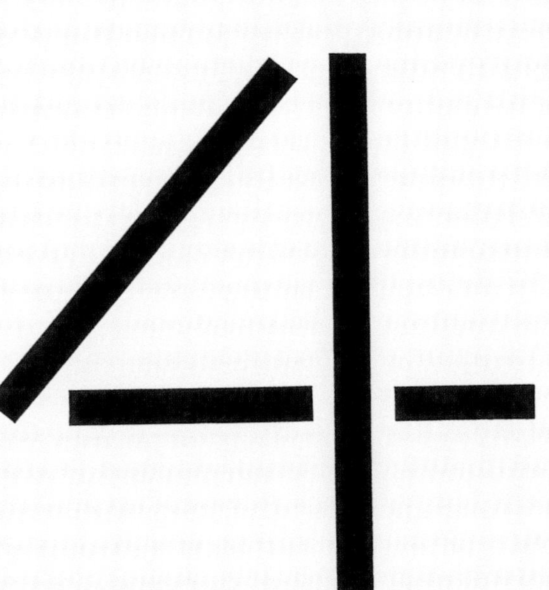

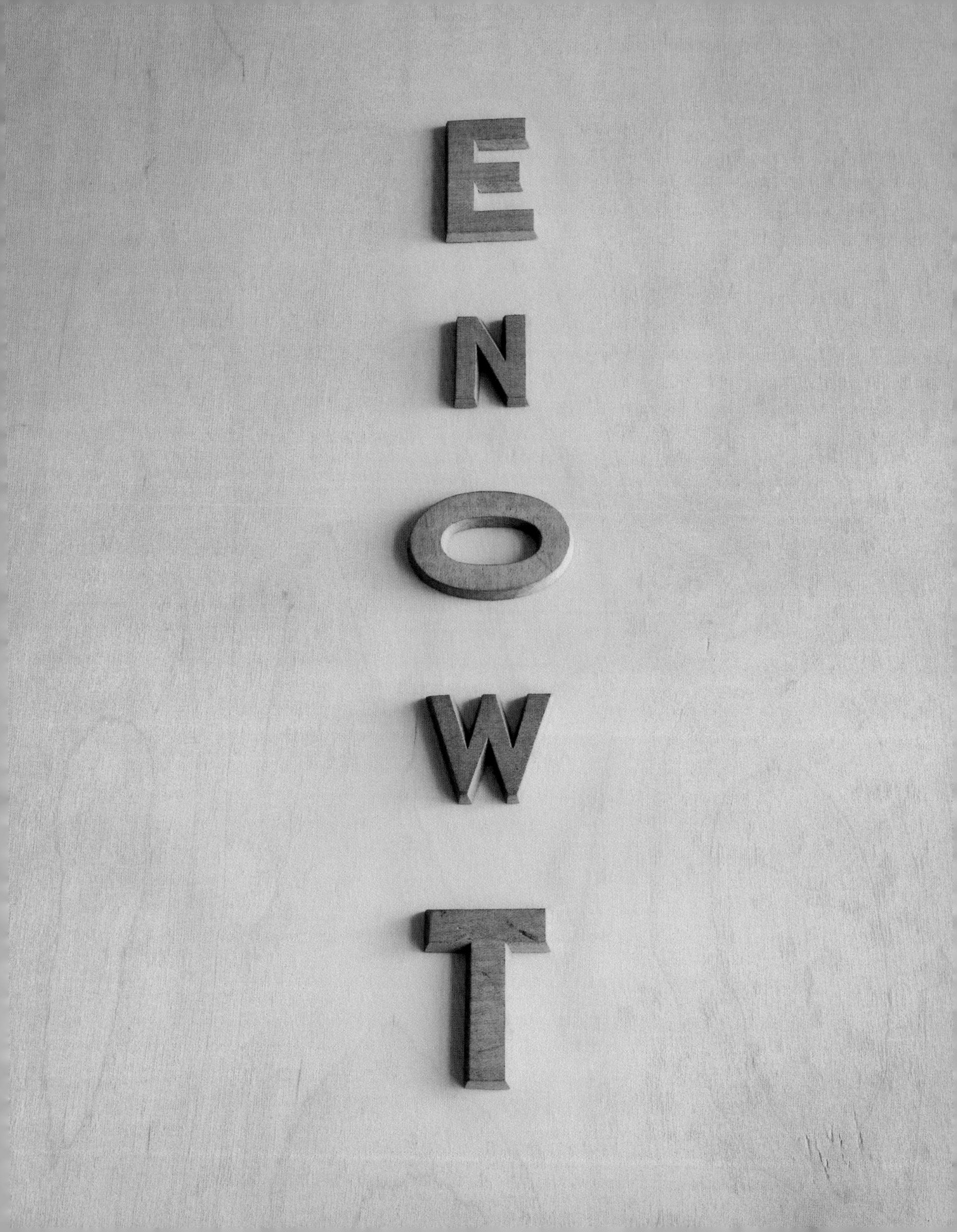

E

N

O

W

T

oooo
oooo

mono
solo

oooooo
ooo

stereo
duo

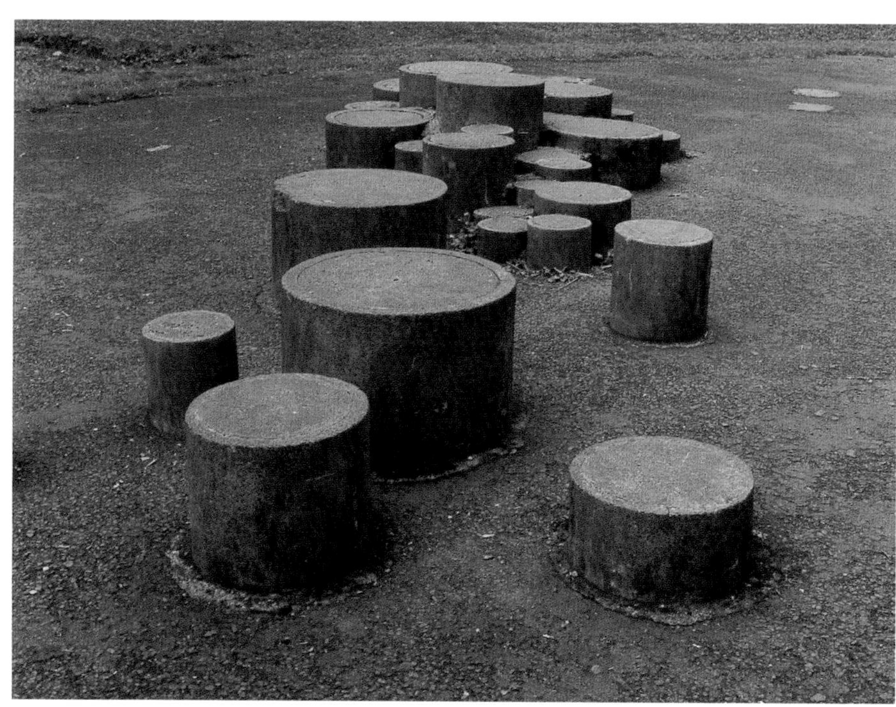

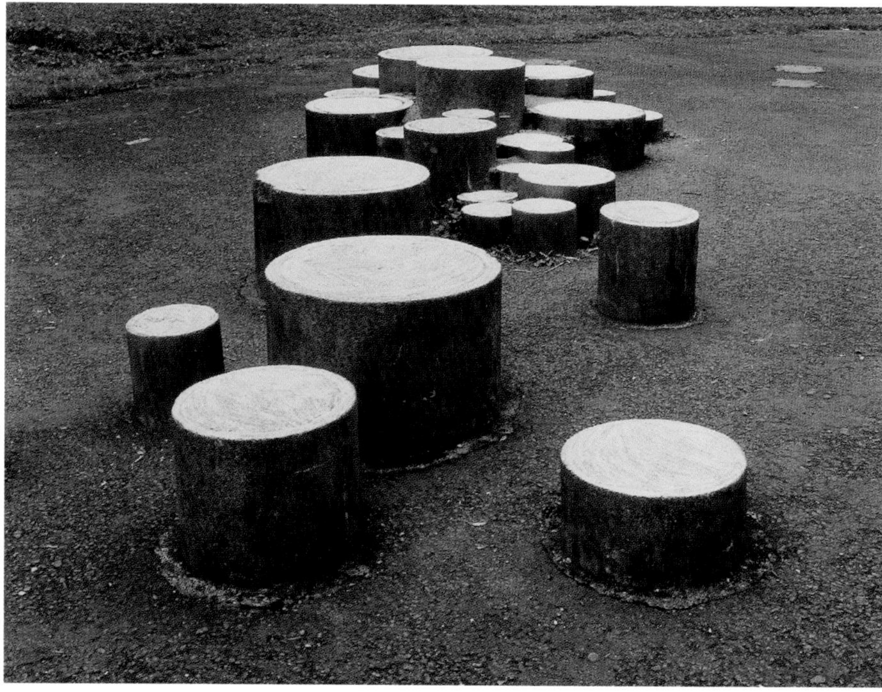

The light of each sentence drawn to conclusion

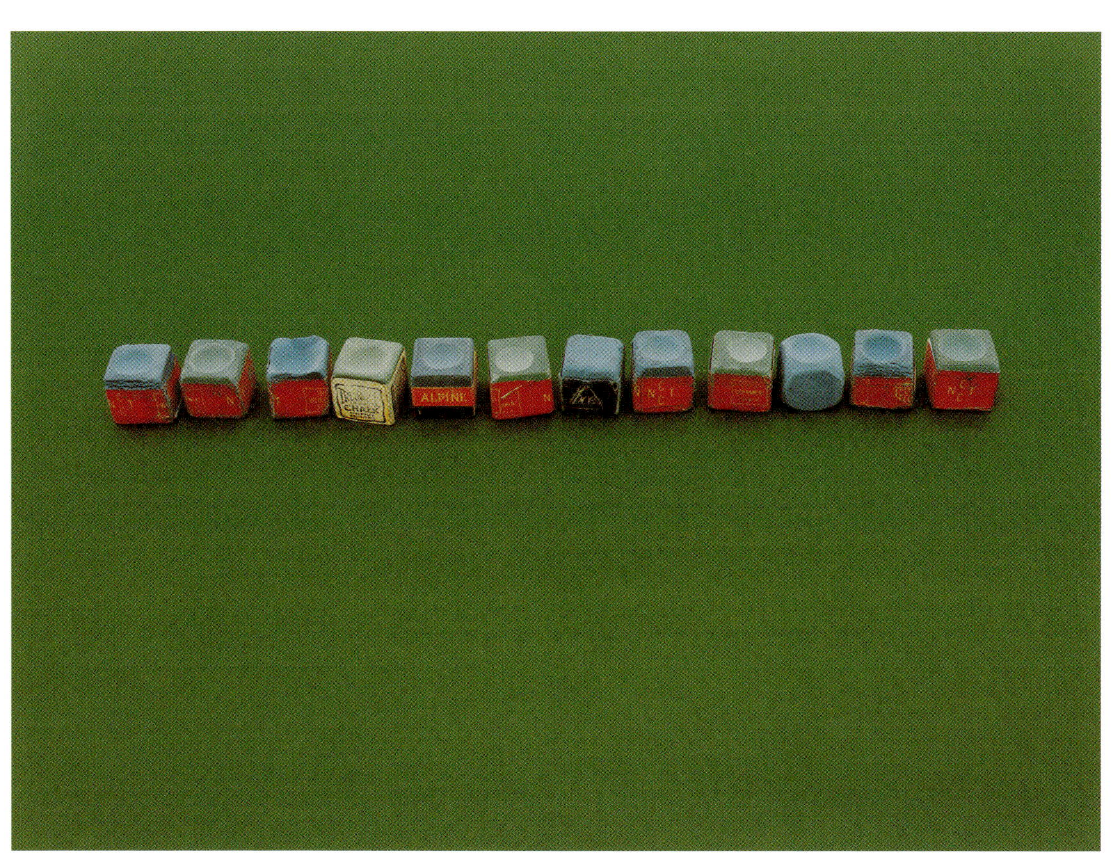

70 Cue Chalk Line (After Yves Klein)

EVERY

OTHER

THING

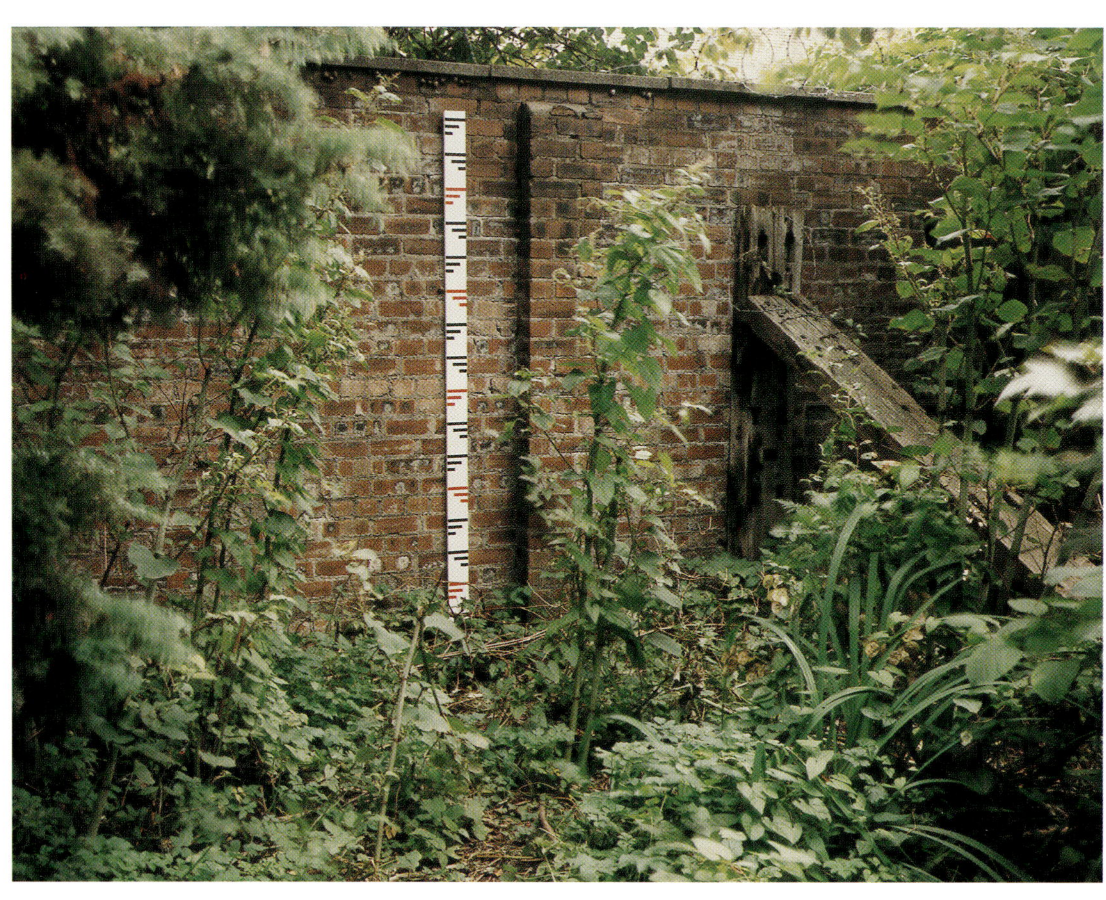

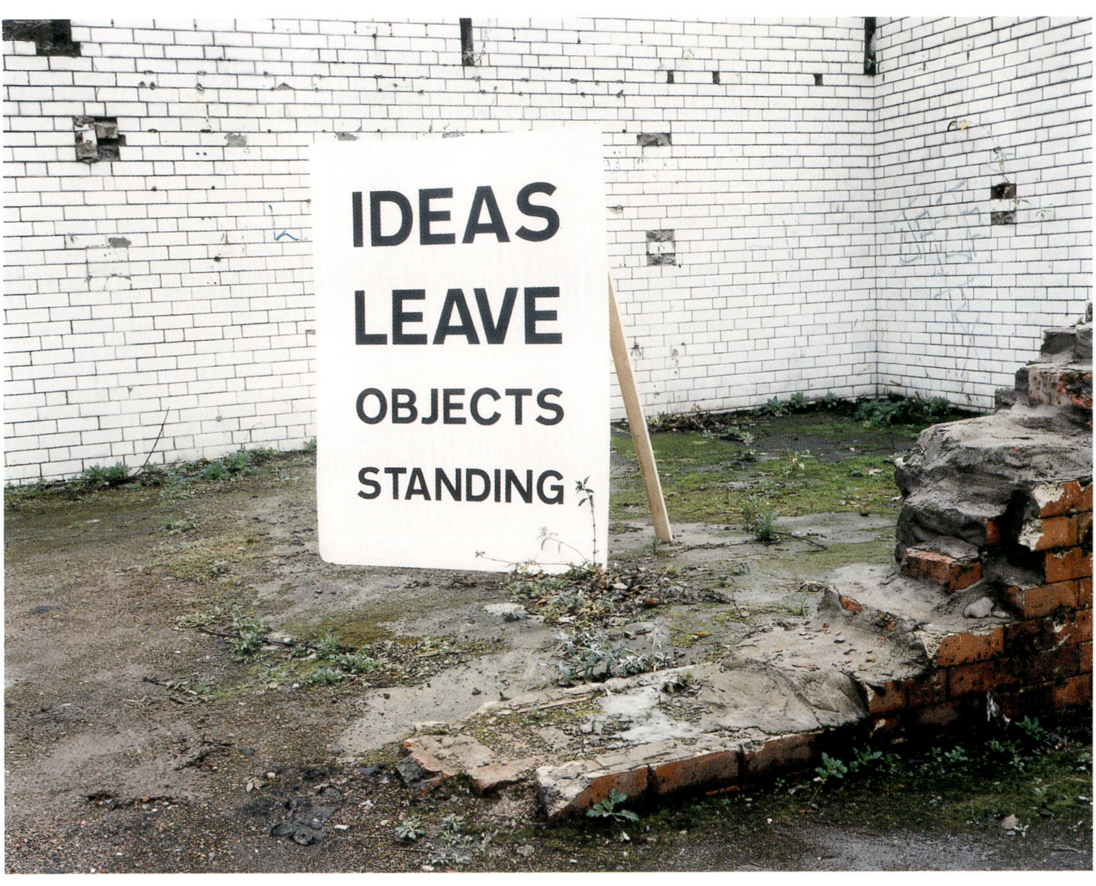
IDEAS
LEAVE
OBJECTS
STANDING

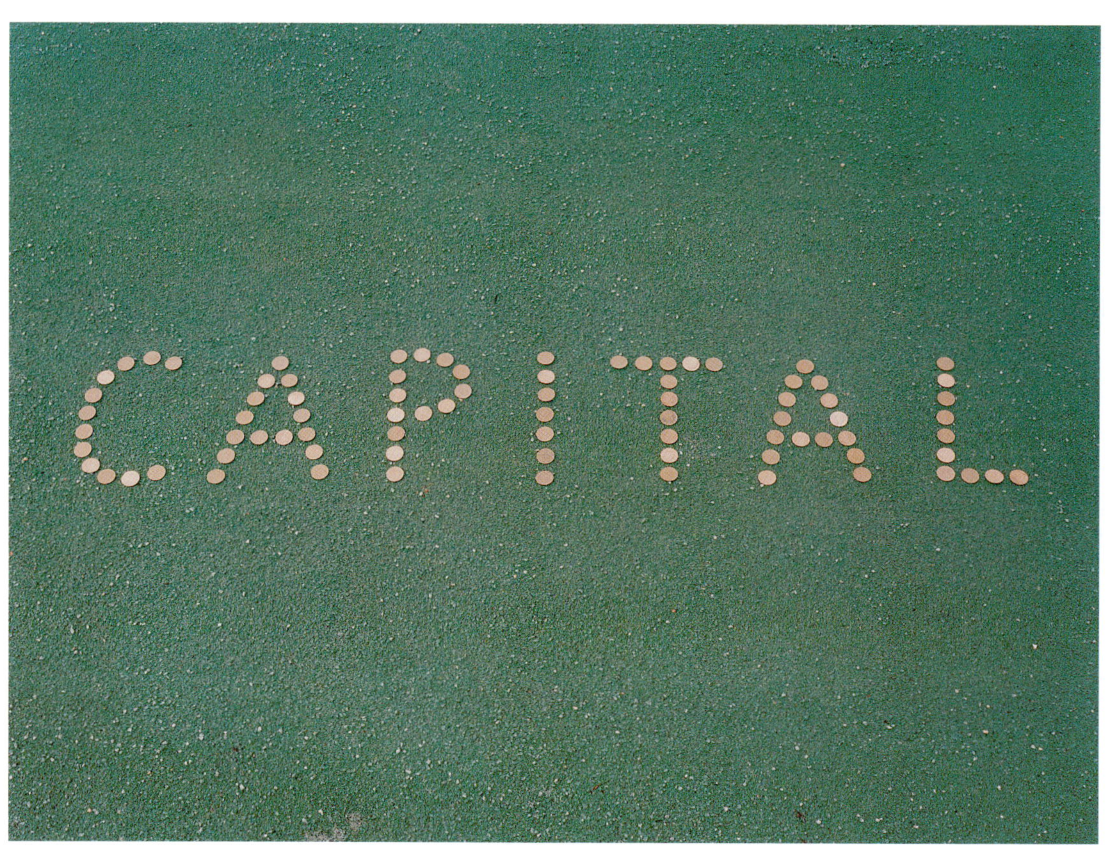
CAPITAL

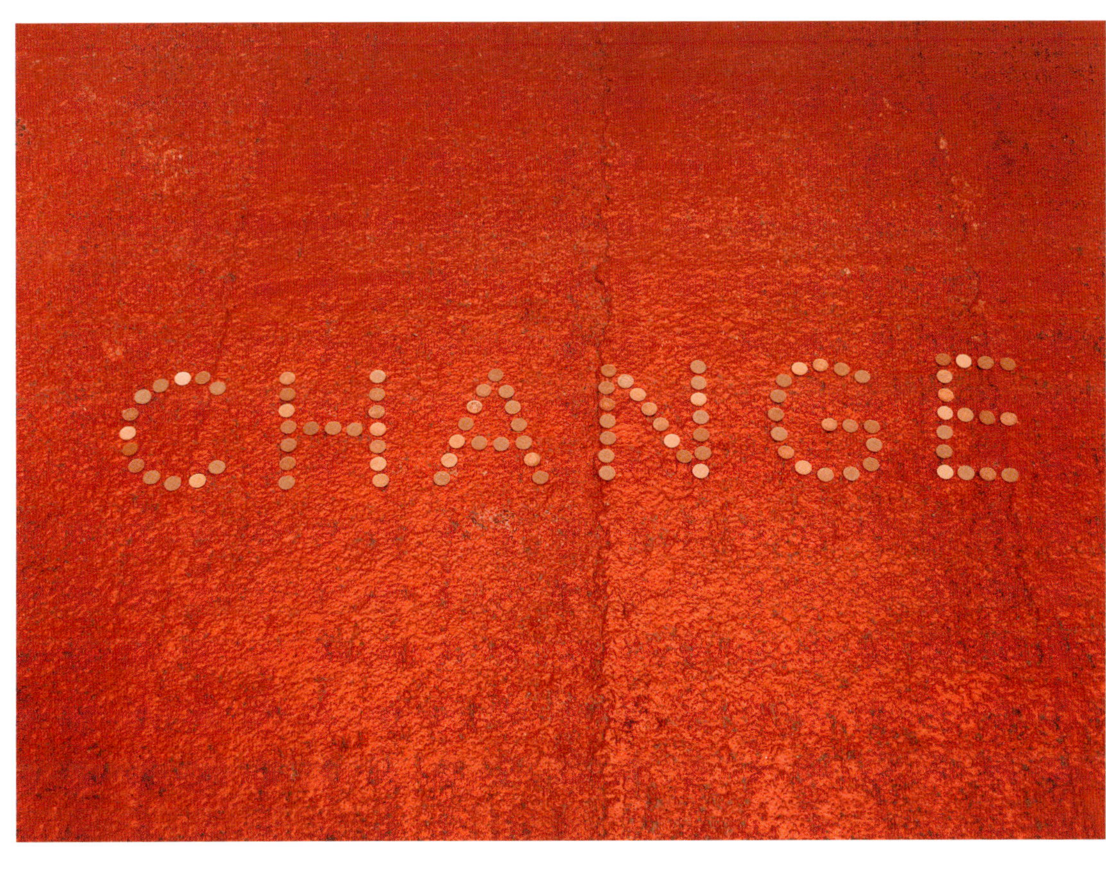
CHANGE

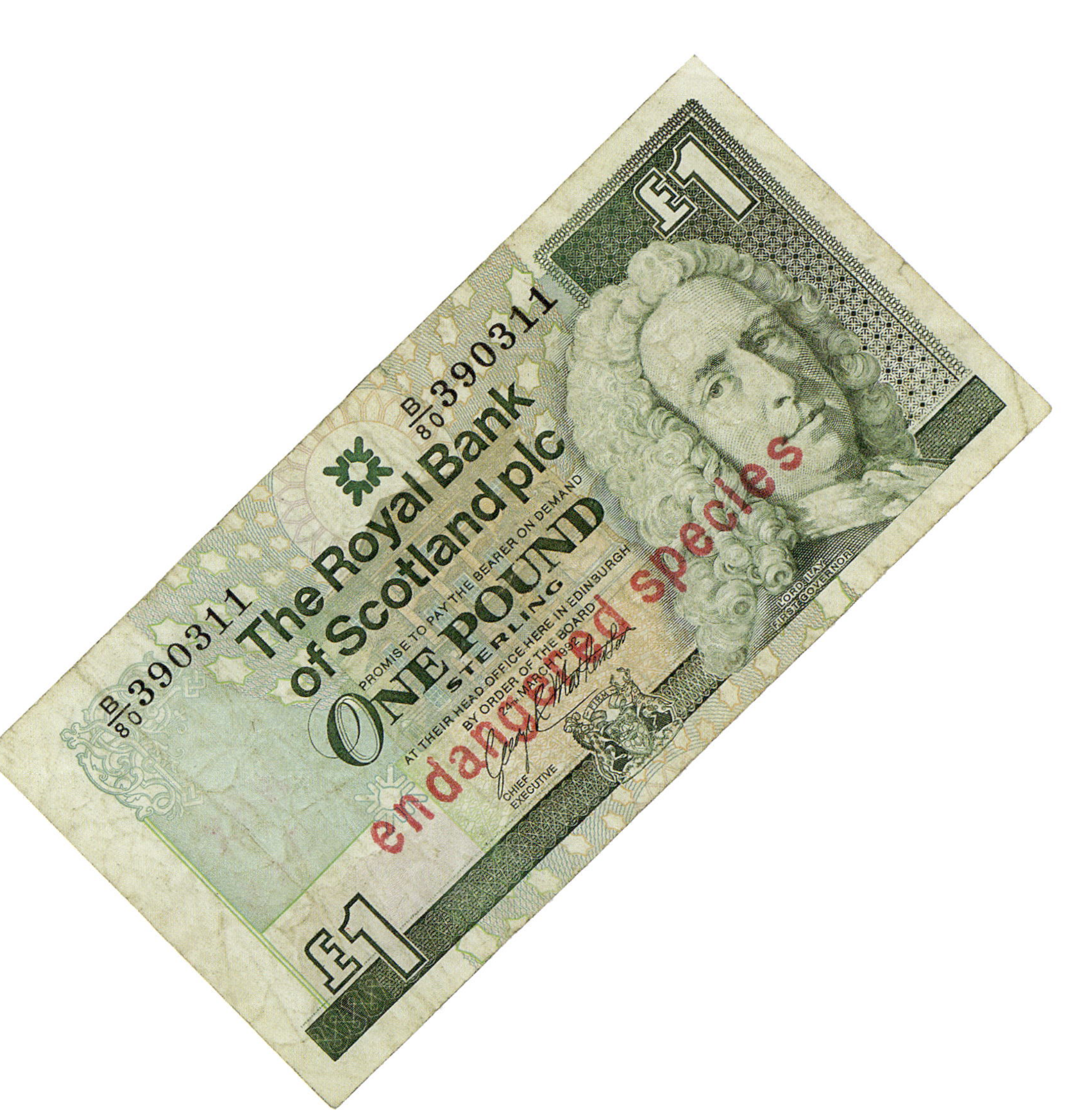
£1
B/80 390311
The Royal Bank
of Scotland plc
PROMISE TO PAY THE BEARER ON DEMAND
ONE POUND
STERLING
AT THEIR HEAD OFFICE HERE IN EDINBURGH
BY ORDER OF THE BOARD
CHIEF EXECUTIVE
LORD ILAY
FIRST GOVERNOR
endangered species
B/80 390311
£1

An executive agency of the Department for Transport, Local Government and the Regions
Driver and Vehicle Licensing Agency, Swansea SA6 7JL Tel: 0870 240 0009

Payment Advice

In all enquiries please quote supplier number below	Payment date	Payable order No.	Amount
999997/00	17/04/2002	1197341	1.00

DAVID ANTHONY BELLINGHAM
60 SALTOUN STREET
GLASGOW
G12 9BE 11332

Your Invoice Reference / Description	Invoice Date	Amount
BELLI612156DA9	17/04/2002	1.00
ONE ONE ONE ONE ONE	ONE ONE	ONE ONE ONE
ONE ONE ONE ONE	ONE ONE	ONE ONE ONE
ONE ONE ONE	ONE ONE	ONE ONE ONE
ONE ONE	ONE ONE	ONE ONE ONE
ONE	ONE ONE	ONE ONE ONE
	ONE ONE	ONE ONE ONE
	ONE	ONE ONE ONE
		ONE ONE ONE
		ONE ONE
		ONE
	Total	1.00

HM Paymaster General RH10 1UH will pay the amount shown if this payable order is presented **within 6 months.**

Issuing Department:
Department for Transport, Local Government and the Regions, DVLA, Longview Road, Morriston, SWANSEA SA6 7JL
Account: DRIVER REFUNDS ACCOUNT

10 million	Million	100,000	10,000	Thousands	Hundreds	Tens	Units
ZERO	ZERO	ZERO	ZERO	ZERO	ZERO	ZERO	ONE

NOT NEGOTIABLE

10-15-83
4949
Date 17/04/2002

Pay to: DAVID ANTHONY BELLINGHAM *or order*

£**1-00**

Reference No: 999997/00
Pay to: 60 SALTOUN STREET
GLASGOW
G12 9BE

Assistant Paymaster General

Printed for SPSL 3162-3188-20609-A16-2/02-9659

⑈004949⑈ 10⑉1583⑆ 1197341⑈

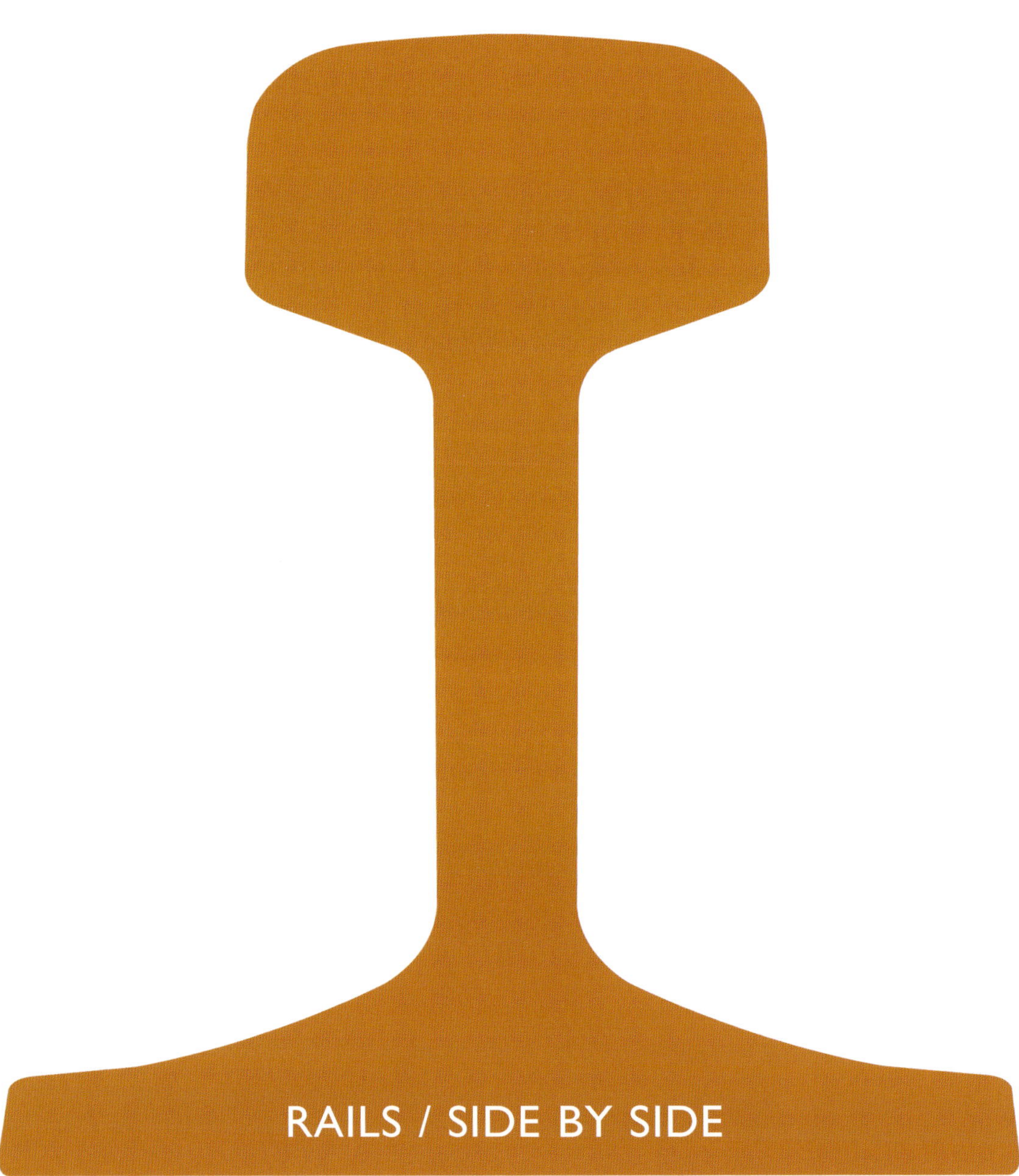
RAILS / SIDE BY SIDE

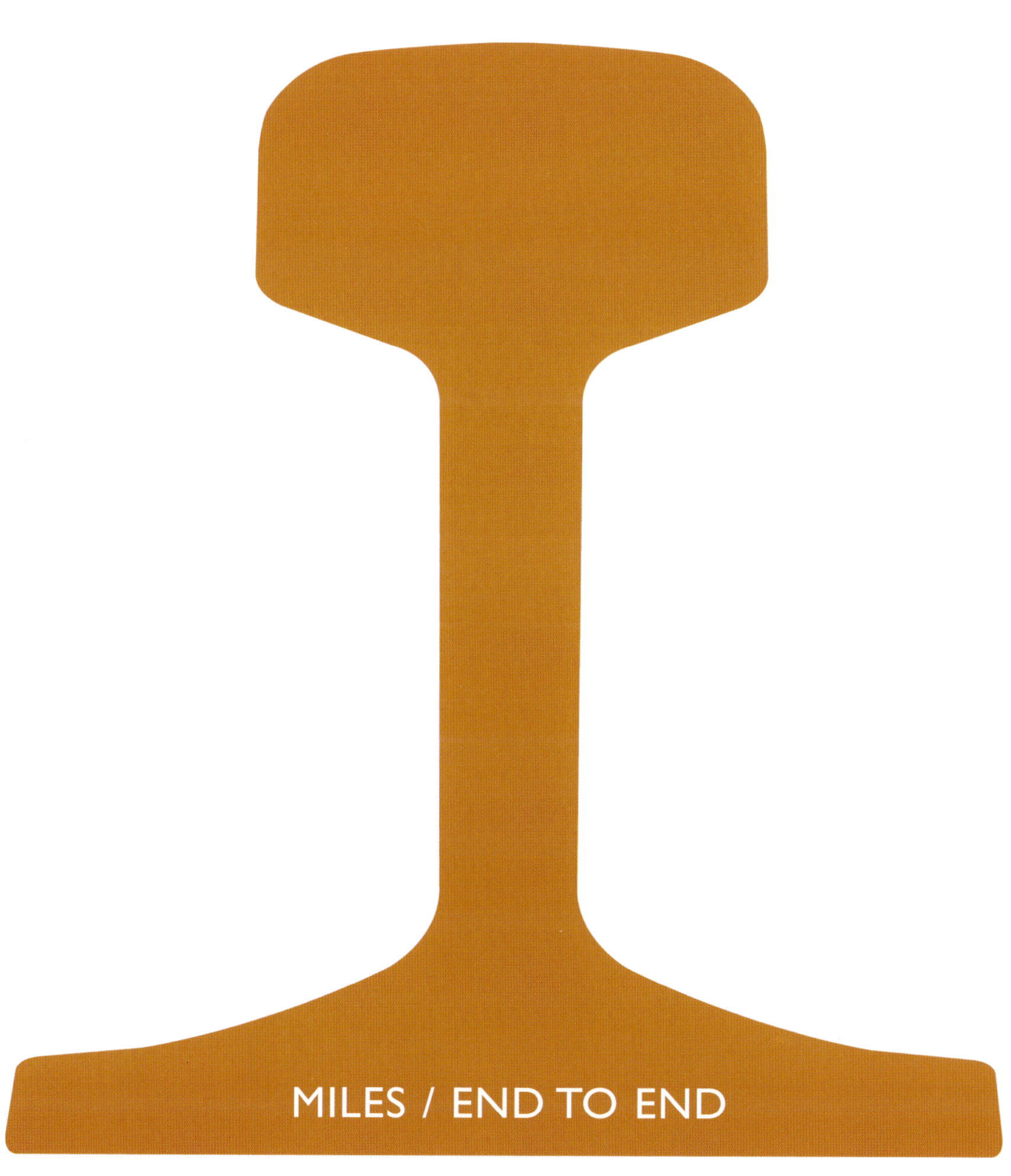
MILES / END TO END

A
A
A
A
A
A
A
A
A
A
A

80 Tensioned to a vanishing point: pylons

the
telegraph
pole

our
national
tree

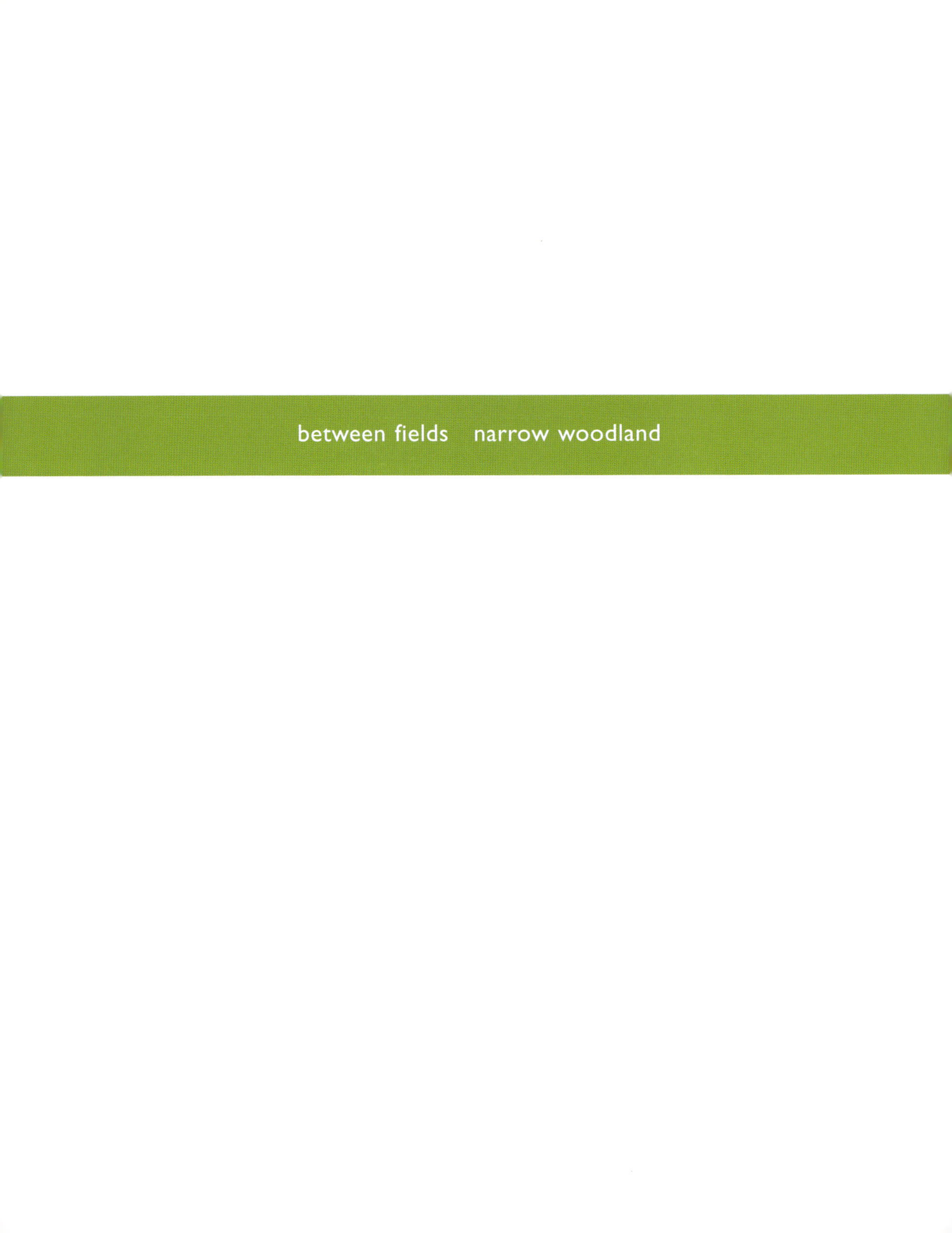
between fields   narrow woodland

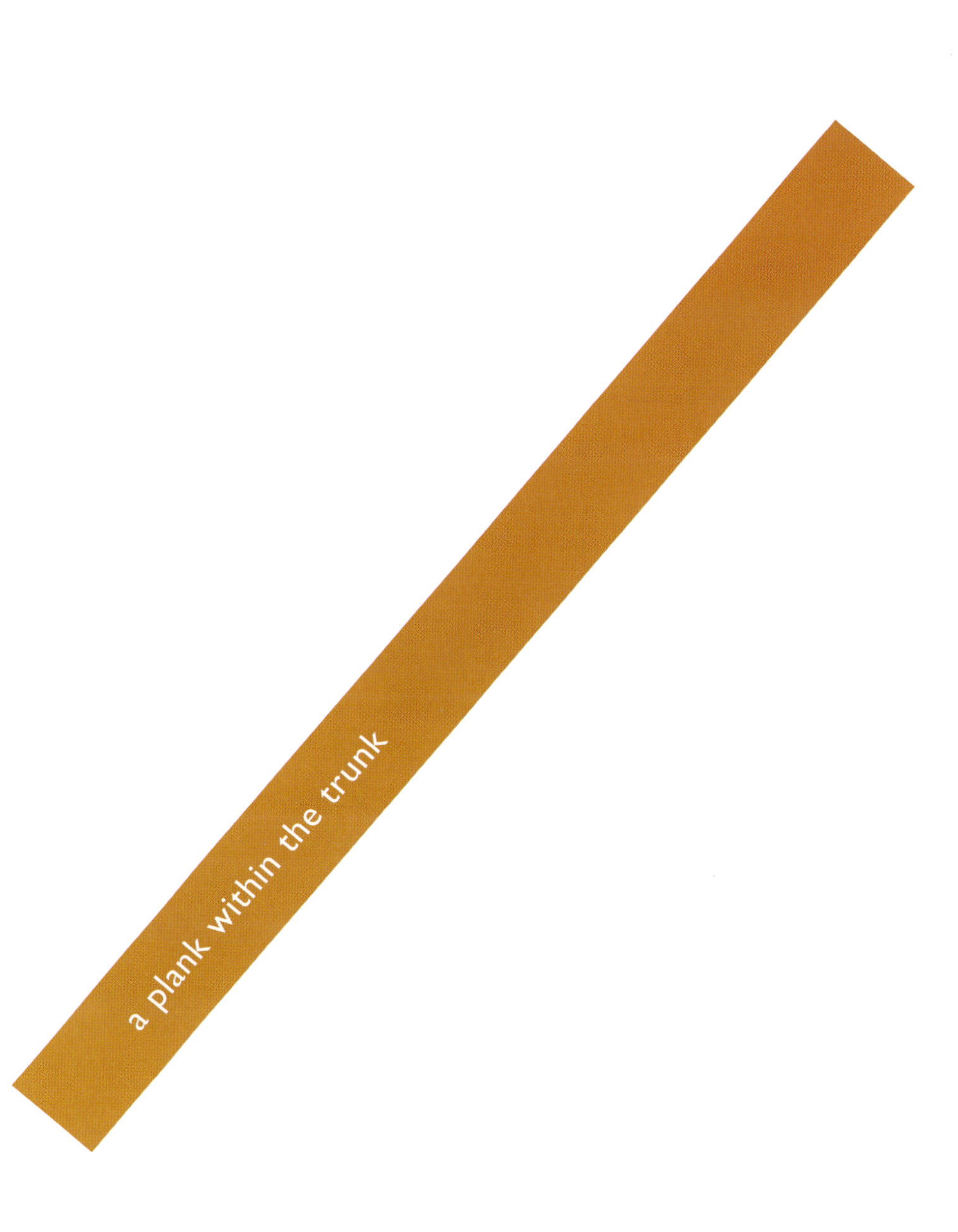
a plank within the trunk

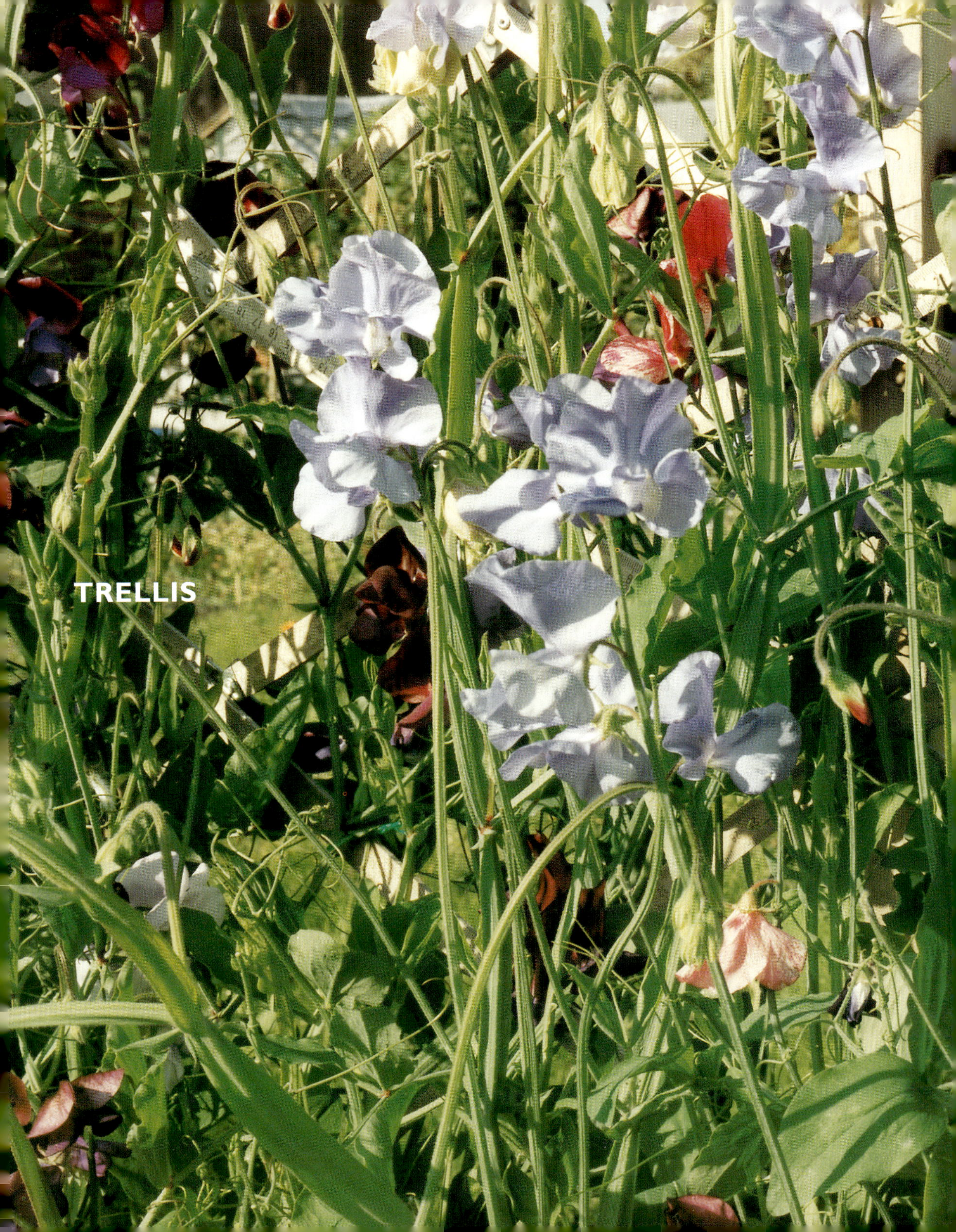
TRELLIS

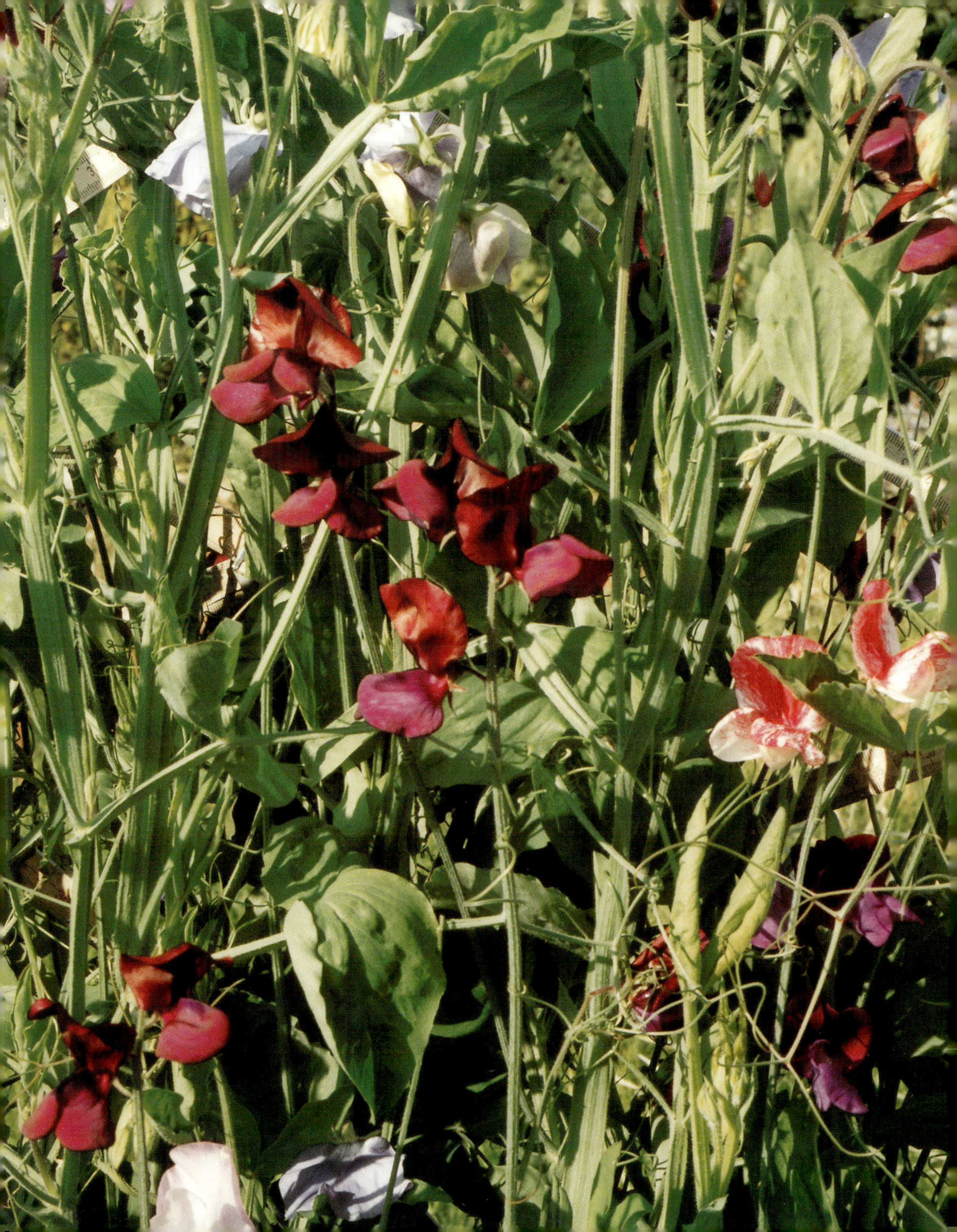

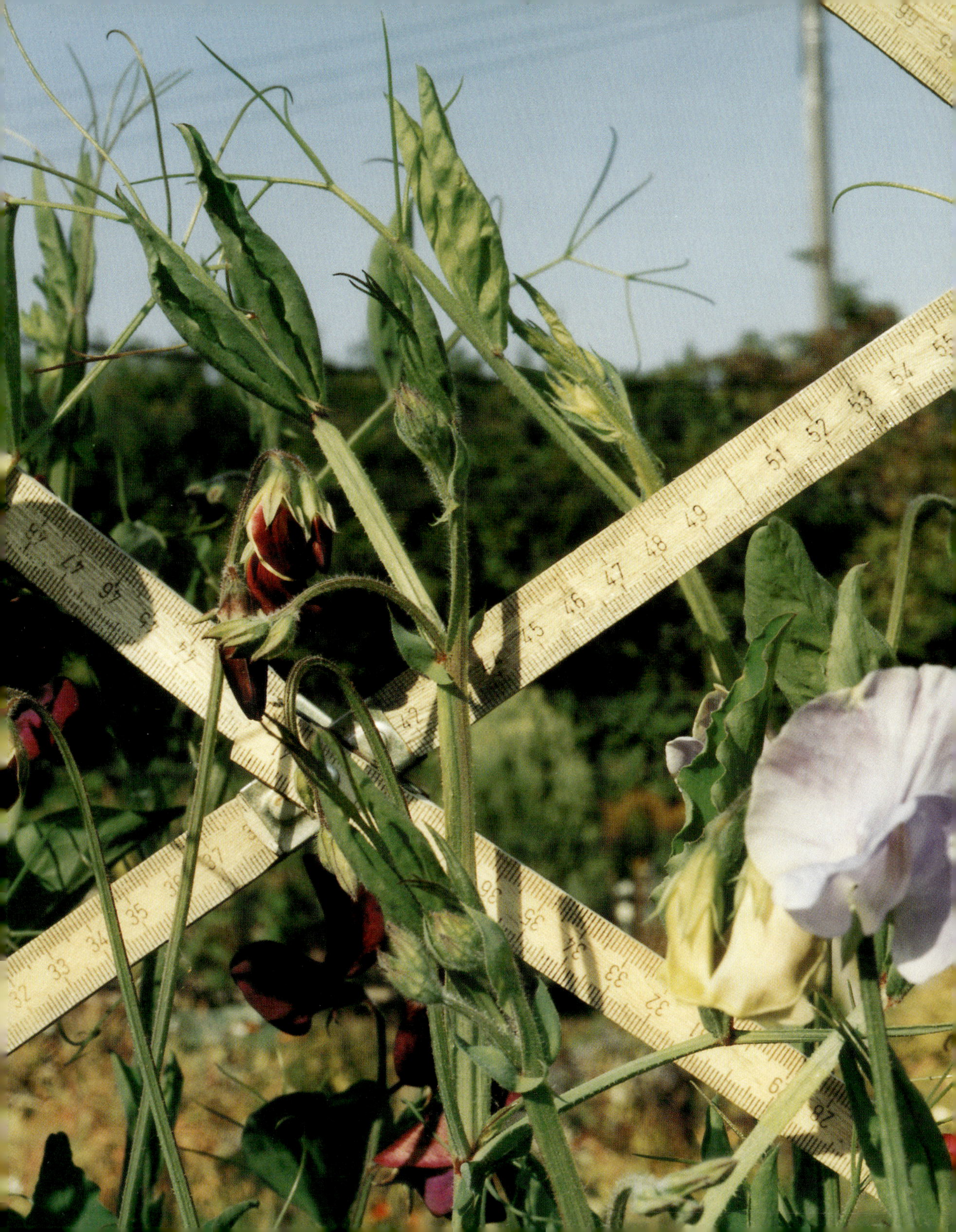

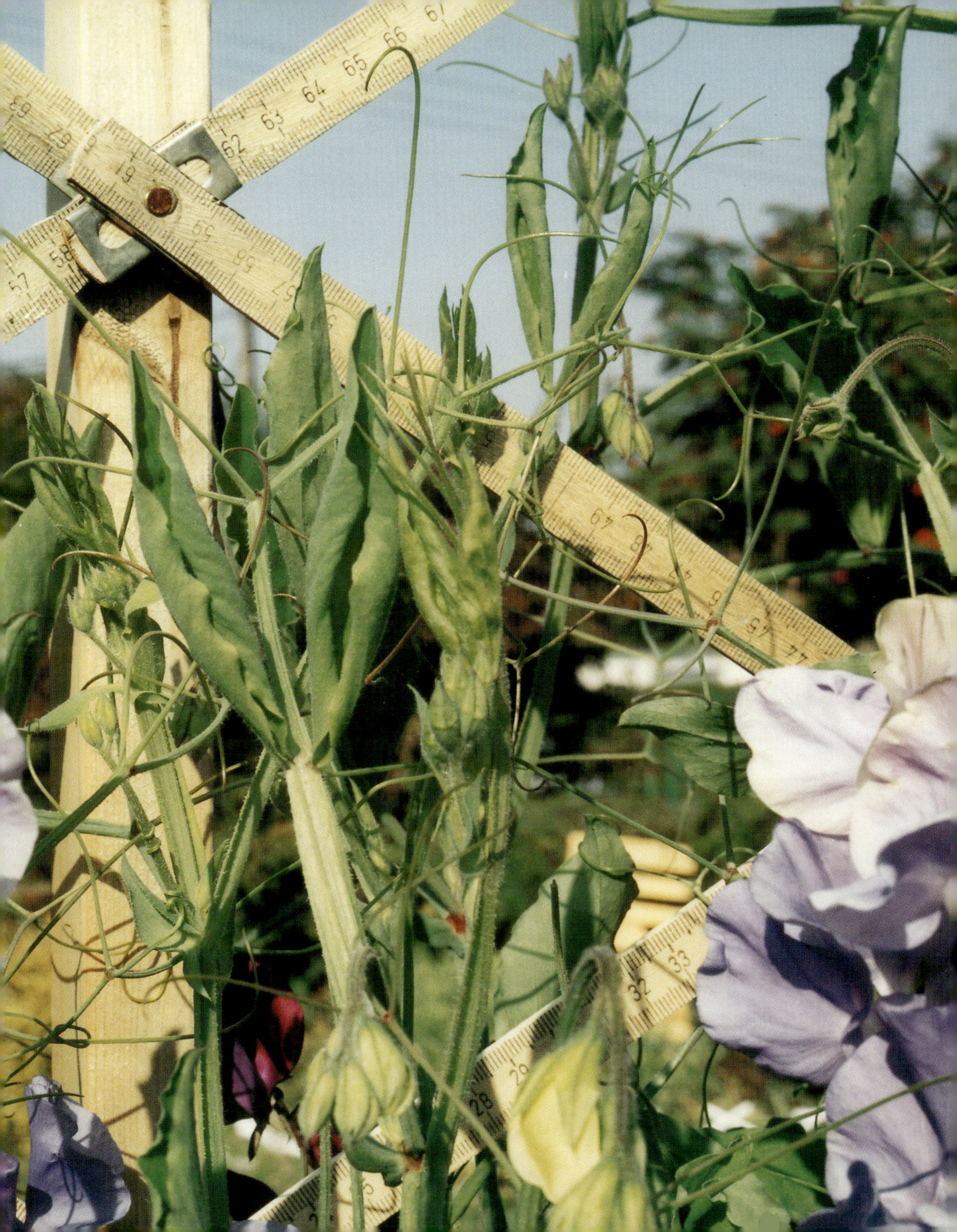

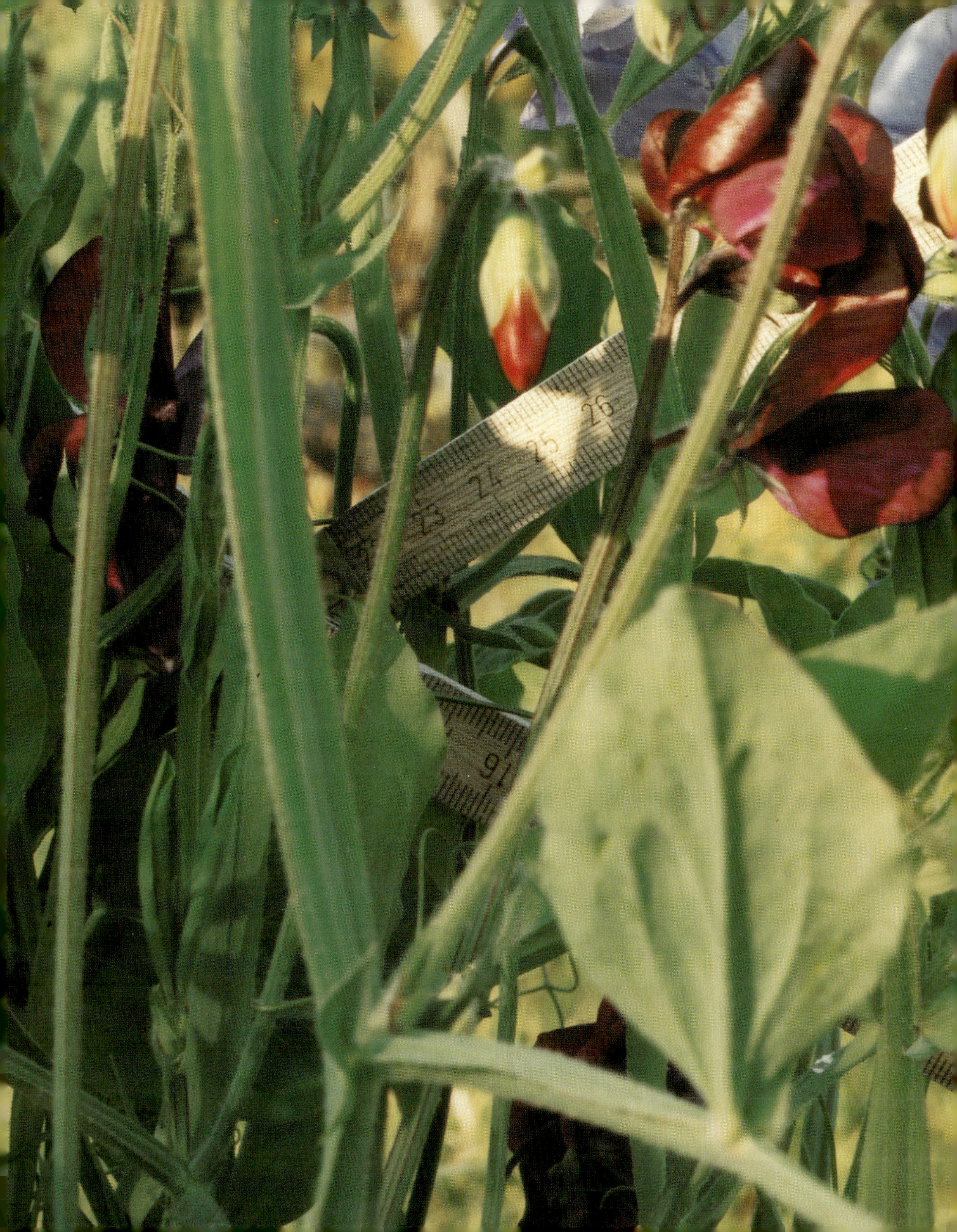
24
25
26

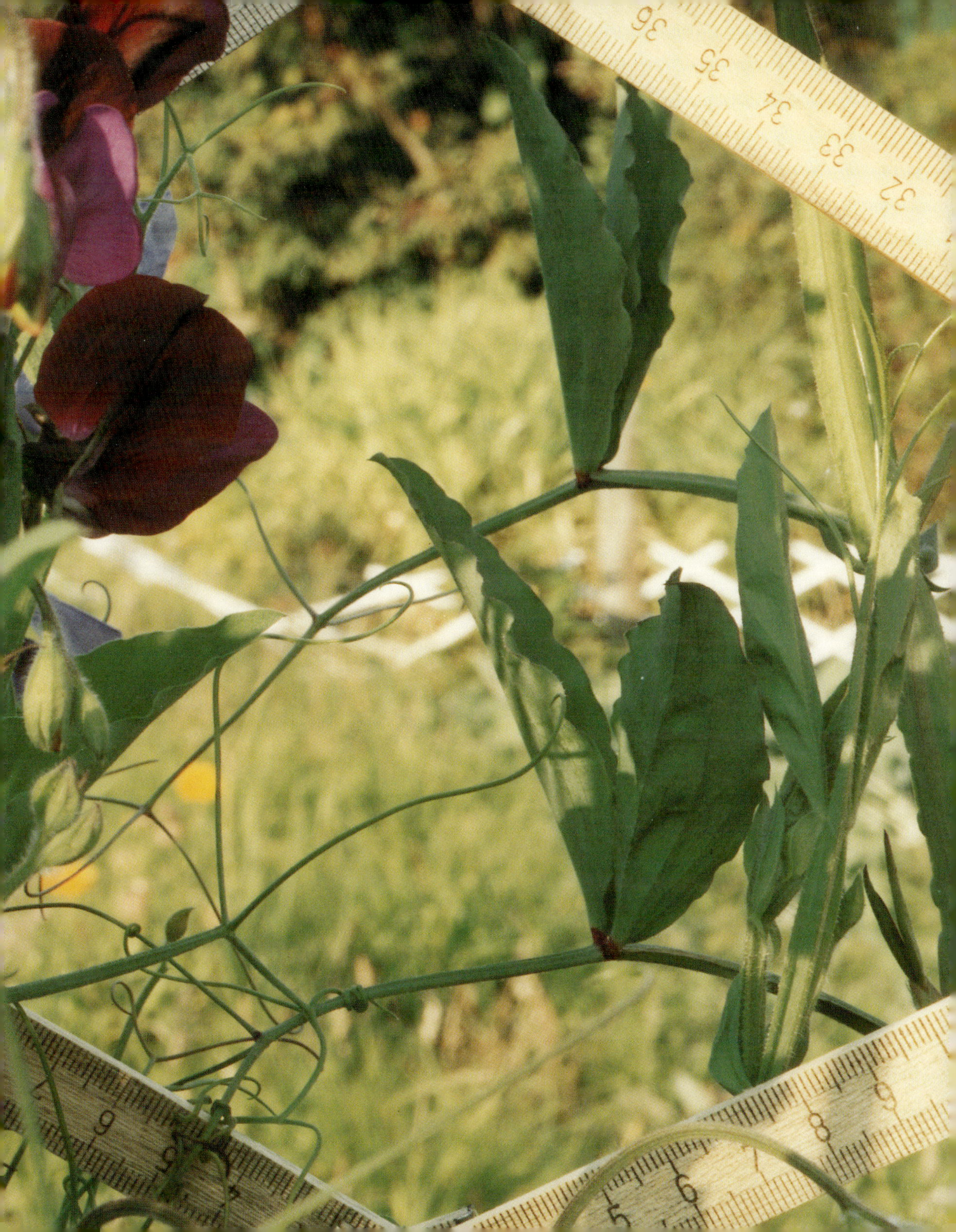

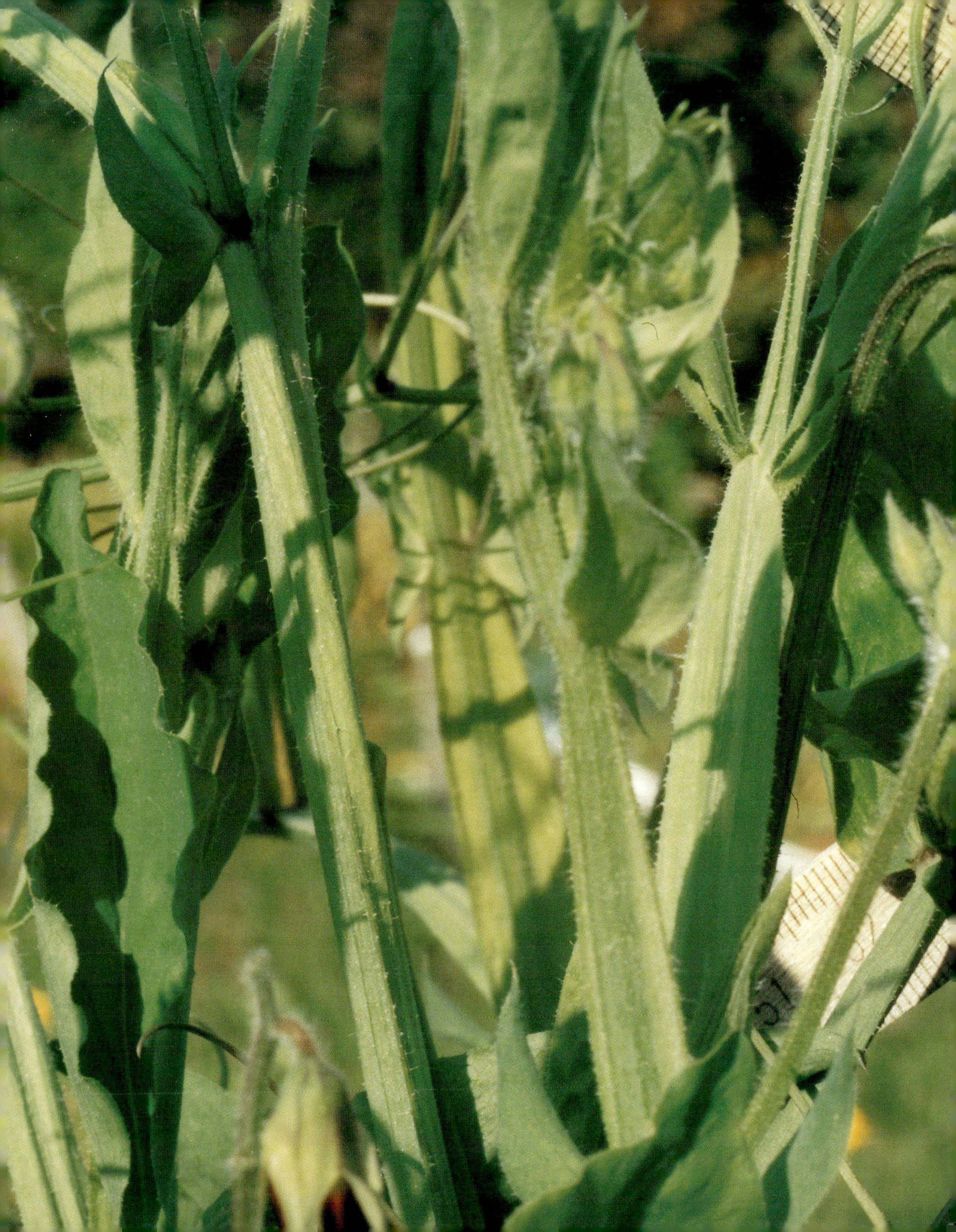

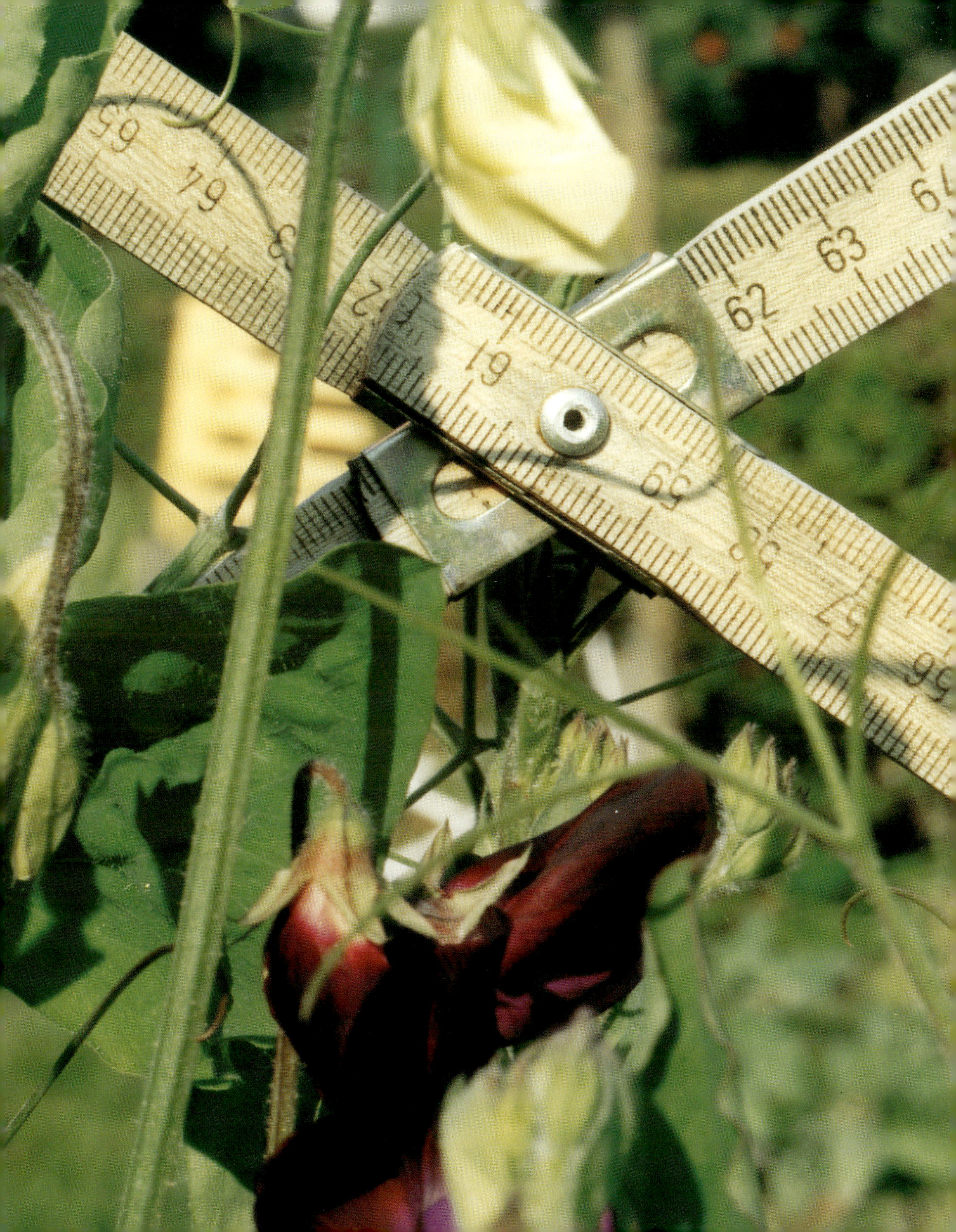

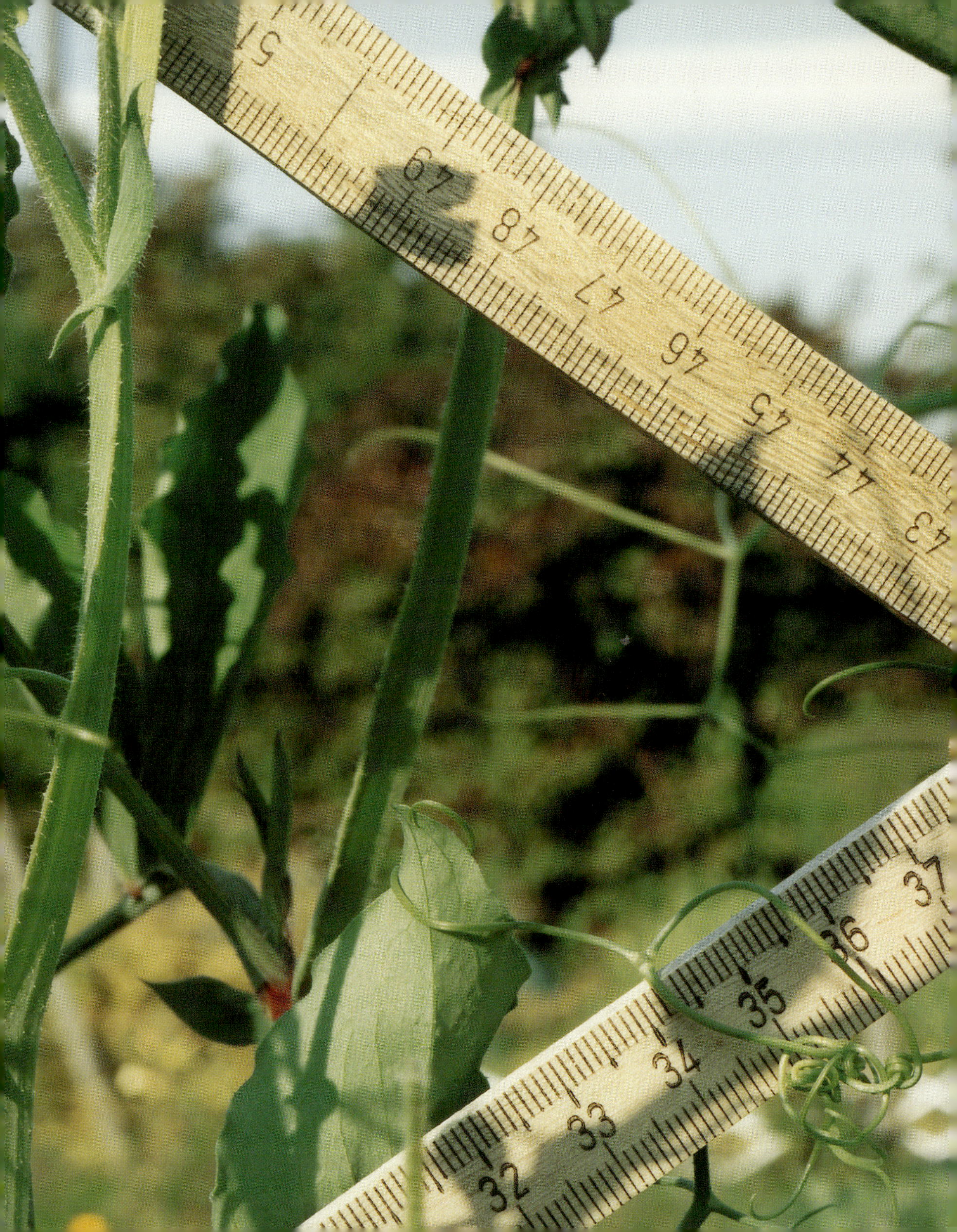

front cover **Ideas Leave Objects Standing** 2003

page 2 **The Three R's** 2004
'Repetition, Repetition, Repetition' Mark E. Smith 1977

page 5 **Just Another Part of The World** 2003, collage 32 x 26cm
'To us and all those who hate us, that the U.S.A. may become just another part of the world, no more no less.' John Cage 1966

page 6 **Cardinal Points** 2002

page 7 **Just Another Part of The World** 2003, photograph 50 x 60cm
Vinyl text on wall

pages 8-9 **Intent / Content** 2003, photographs 50 x 60cm

pages 10-11 **Citrus Finials** 2003, photographs 50 x 60cm

pages 12-13 **Lemon Yellow Lemon** 1996

pages 14-15 **Collage I + II (after Jiří Kolář)** 2004
photographs 18 x 18cm

page 18 **Atlantic Wall** 2001, photograph 50 x 60cm

page 19 **Digits** 2001, photograph 20 x 25.5cm

page 21 **Cruise** 1998
A definition to mark four nights of airstrikes in the Gulf.
First published as a postcard in December 1998 by WAX366

page 22 **Autumn 2001**
First published as a photocopied document of 12 pages

page 23 **green field / brown field / oil field / battle field** 2002
First published as a broadsheet by WAX366

page 24 **The Meek Shall Inherit The Map** 2003, collage 32 x 26cm

page 25 **Keep the Flags Furled** 2002, collage 32 x 26cm

pages 26-27 **Paper Aeroplanes** 1999, photographs 50 x 60cm

page 28 **Composition In Red, Yellow & Green** 2001, photograph 20 x 25.5cm
Reducible Foot 2002, chocolate bar with wrapper, edition 150 WAX366

page 29 **Workplace 3** 2002, photograph 50 x 60cm

pages 30-31 **Configurations of Three** 2004, two collages 32 x 24 cm, ed 5

pages 32-33 From the book **Continuous Lines** 2002-3

page 34 **Black Blanc** 2002, photograph 50 x 60cm

page 35 **Not Only Black & White** 2001, photograph 50 x 60cm

page 36-37 **Over / Under** 2000, two photographs 50 x 60cm

page 38 **From One Language To Another** 2000

page 39 **Table of Contents** 2001

page 40 **Over Heard / Over Head** 2003

page 41 **A Weight of Words As Light As Paper** 2002
First published as a broadsheet by WAX366

page 42 **Morning / Evening / Daily** 2003, collage 60 x 50cm

page 43 **Daily / Weekly** 2003, collage 60 x 50cm

page 45 **Mont Blanc** 2001, photograph 25 x 16cm, with Anne Bjerge Hansen

page 46-55 Texts for pages and walls

page 56 **Open / Closed** 2004, drawing 30 x 21cm

page 57 **Things Over Signs** 2003

pages 58-59 **working / playing** from the series **returns** 2002-4
Vinyl text on walls, photographs 50 x 60cm

pages 60-61 **javelin / discus / shot-put** 2003
Typed page and drawing, each 32 x 22.5cm

pages 62-63 **Triangle / Square** 2003
Triangle and adapted triangle, edition of 20 WAX366

Thank you:
Anne, Andy, The Burryman, Cluny, David, Eck, Harry, Hugh, Jim, Klaus, Kurt, Laurie, Lucy, Pavel, Roger, Tatiana, Thomas, Tom.

A platform projects book
Designed by David Bellingham and Lucy Richards

Published by Platform Projects:
21A West Mayfield
Edinburgh, EH9 1TQ

BALTIC The Centre for Contemporary Art
South Shore Road, Gateshead NE8 3BA
www.balticmill.com

Printed by Graphicom, Italy

The publishers acknowledge support from the Scottish Arts Council towards the publication of this title

Glasgow School of Art
A.H.R.B.

Edition 1,500 copies

ISBN 0 9546831 5 3